THE SHADOW KNOWS

There is a shadow lurking in every person's inner life, a psychic darkness sheltering our inner conflicts and unexpressed emotions. It takes its shape from a menagerie of archetypes, each recognizable throughout time and around the world—troubling characters who thrive within our persona. The shadow is the saboteur, martyr, victim, addict, sadist, masochist, or tyrant, all the dark figures that prey on the lighter qualities of the human personality.

The shadow also represents those latent talents and positive traits that were banished from us at some time along our life path: artistic, musical, athletic, or creative talents. An undeveloped ability, a dream that has gone unexpressed, a fantasy of what might have been—these, too, make up the personal shadow, the lost parts of ourselves.

To channel the negative characters in our personality, we first must bring them into our waking consciousness. *Tarot Shadow Work* will help you come to terms with life's dualities, show you how to embrace the darkness, and teach you how to balance the light with the shadow in your own life. The entire world of the human psyche can be mapped out using the twenty-two cards of the tarot's major arcana, with each card tapping into a different quality of our psychology.

Accepting that we are made of both light and darkness, life will start to make sense. When we accept our dual natures, we stop sabotaging our own efforts and learn to be compassionate with others and with ourselves.

About the Author

Christine Jette (pronounced "Jetty") is a registered nurse and holds a bachelor of arts degree in psychology. She is a therapeutic touch practitioner and professional tarot consultant. Christine specializes in health readings combined with hands-on (energetic) healing. She teaches professional writing part-time at the University of Cincinnati and lives in Cincinnati with her husband and two (spoiled) cats.

To Write to the Author

If you wish to contact the author or would like more information about this book, please write to the author in care of Llewellyn Worldwide and we will forward your request. Both the author and publisher appreciate hearing from you and learning of your enjoyment of this book and how it has helped you. Llewellyn Worldwide cannot guarantee that every letter written to the author can be answered, but all will be forwarded. Please write to:

Christine Jette
℅ Llewellyn Worldwide
P.O. Box 64383, Dept. K408-1
St. Paul, MN 55164-0383, U.S.A.

Please enclose a self-addressed stamped envelope for reply, or $1.00 to cover costs. If outside U.S.A., enclose international postal reply coupon.

Many of Llewellyn's authors have websites with additional information and resources. For more information, please visit our website at http://www.llewellyn.com

TAROT
SHADOW WORK
USING THE DARK SYMBOLS TO HEAL

CHRISTINE JETTE

2000
Llewellyn Publications
St. Paul, Minnesota 55164-0383, U.S.A.

First Edition
First Printing, 2000

Book design by Kimberly Nightingale
Cover design by Lisa Novak
Cover photo by Doug Deutcher
Edited by Tom Lewis
Tarot cards from *The Robin Wood Tarot*, by Robin Wood (Llewellyn, 1991)

Library of Congress Cataloging-in-Publication Data
    Jette, Christine, 1953–
        Tarot shadow work : using the dark symbols to heal / Christine Jette.— 1st ed.
            p. cm.
    Includes bibliographical references and index.
    ISBN 1-56718-408-1
        1. Tarot. 2. Shadow (Psychoanalysis)—Miscellanea.   I. Title.

BF1879.T2 J44 2000
133.3'2424—dc21

                                                                        00-044406

Llewellyn Publications
A Division of Llewellyn Worldwide, Ltd.
P.O. Box 64383, Dept. K408-1
St. Paul, MN 55164-0383, U.S.A.
www.llewellyn.com

 Printed in the United States of America on Recycled Paper

Forthcoming by Christine Jette:

Tarot for the Healing Heart
(July 2001)

For Kate

CONTENTS

PART I: THE SHADOW KNOWS

PART II: INTO THE LIGHT

PART III: STAR GUIDES

T̊AROT ꟅPREADS

Acknowledgments

*You shall bring forth your work
as a mother brings forth her child:
from the blood of your heart.*
Gabriela Mistral

The process of birthing a book is a daunting task and cannot be accomplished alone. I wish to gratefully acknowledge the guidance and support I received along my journey. Thanks to:

Tim, my husband and best friend.

My therapist Kathleen—led by the courage of Leo, I explored my own dark shadows.

The wonderful staff at Llewellyn—giving of time and expertise. Thanks especially to: Barbara Wright, Nancy J. Mostad, Megan Atwood, and Ann Kerns for their support; Lisa Novak for the beautiful cover; Lisa Braun in Publicity; Kimberly Nightingale for the interior design; and last, but certainly not least, Tom Lewis, my editor (aka "The Words Guy").

Because of you, my book is better. Thanks to you all!

Prologue

DUSK

I WAS RAISED ON A LARGE OHIO FARM IN A TRADITIONAL FAMILY STRUC-
ture—mother, father, older sister. I met my first dark shadow at the age
of fourteen. Its name was anorexia nervosa. Despite the illness, I was
valedictorian of my high school class. Graduation day was a happy time.
I could not predict the descent into darkness that lay before me.

While in college, I met two more shadows. Their names were alcoholism and drug addiction. Not yet conscious of their power, I was
swept into a downward spiral of self-destruction. I found myself in a
physically abusive first marriage and here I met the fourth shadow—my
willingness to be a victim. I felt controlled by nameless, powerful forces.
My life was a frightening place.

After my divorce, I spiraled deeper and was taken to a psychiatric
hospital by my family. It was 1983 and I was thirty years old. While hos-
pitalized, I was introduced to psychotherapy and the concept of shadow.
The horrible things happening to me had names and I had a personal
responsibility to acquaint myself with them. It was up to me to take
charge of my own recovery. After years of struggling, I was informed I

had a choice. I could choose to live . . . or not. There was no way over, under, or around the shadow. The only path to freedom was through the darkness.

It was slow, painful work, but I discovered the shadow had a purpose. It carried messages about my personal growth. It pointed me to where I had been hurt and what I needed to examine. My life started making sense.

In this book, I define "shadow" as a person's unresolved inner conflicts and unexpressed emotions. Drawing on the experience of my own losses, I began to develop the idea of shadow work using tarot cards.

Tarot Shadow Work is a culmination of that endeavor; using the methods found here, inner conflicts can find resolution, unexpressed emotions can find a voice. Change occurs because of the power of choice. Choice leads to healing and the gift of healing is creative freedom.

The goal of this workbook is acceptance and integration of the shadow, not its rejection. What are the messages carried by your shadow? What is the shadow trying to convey to you about your personal growth? By understanding your own humanity you can extend that insight to others and know compassion.

I hope *Tarot Shadow Work* opens a new chapter in the story of your life. May it bring peace and healing to all souls in pain.

PART I

THE SHADOW KNOWS

Chapter 1
NIGHTFALL

One does not discover new lands without
losing sight of the shore for a very long time.
Andre Gide

The Shadow in Literature and Myth

PETER PAN HAD LOST HIS SHADOW. WENDY SEWED IT BACK ON BECAUSE he couldn't exist without it. References to the shadow are found in literature, myth, the Bible, and common English expressions: "a shadowy figure," "the valley of the shadow of death," "a shadow of your former self," a detective "shadows" his suspect, and so on. All the phrases carry a hint of something mysterious, fearful, misunderstood, incomplete, or possibly even dysfunctional.

We are both fascinated and appalled by the shadow in literature. Dr. Jekyll's alter ego, Mr. Hyde, is a menace. Dracula at once represents sexual desire and evil without end. Werewolves are good men by day, brutal beasts at the full moon. We are exposed to a despairing view of life in *Hamlet*, as the Prince of Denmark proclaims, "Life's but a walking shadow, a poor player/ That struts and frets his hour upon the stage/ And then is heard no more . . ." (Act V, Scene 5, lines 24–26) Even Superman must hide his exceptional qualities behind his shadow self, Clark Kent.

Pan, in Greek mythology, was god of forests, pastures, flocks, and shepherds. He was shunned by the other gods for his ugliness. His music, played unseen in a dark cave, was alluring—but he has come to represent the shadowy parts of ourselves we would rather not know.

Also from Greece, the goddess Hecate took the form of a wise-woman crone, keeper of the mysteries at the gateway to the Underworld. She could see the past, present, and future at once, and was the goddess of prophecy. Hecate was the overseer of the spiral of life in death and rebirth. Today she has been transformed into an ugly old green hag with warts, the wicked witch of Halloween—the shadow side of aging, lost beauty, the unknowable, and death.

The Book of Revelation describes a war in heaven. The angels revolt because Lucifer, the "Bearer of Light," ambitiously tries to usurp his Creator's power. He is cast out of heaven by the Archangel Michael and becomes the Christian Devil. This embodiment of evil symbolizes the most powerful shadow of all—unresolved fear.

When we are separated from our shadow we become a Peter Pan: emotionally immature, unable to face reality, trapped in wishful thinking, unwilling to grow. You can avoid the Peter Pan syndrome by embracing your shadow and the opportunities it offers. *Tarot Shadow Work* will show you how.

Why Bring Up a Dead Psychiatrist?

The Swiss psychiatrist Carl Jung was a thinker ahead of his time. Born on July 26, 1875, his groundbreaking work in depth psychology laid the foundation for contemporary ways of seeing the world. When we use the common terms introvert, extrovert, persona, feeling state, collective unconscious, complex, or archetype, we are quoting Carl Jung. When we talk of the symbolism of myths, dreams, tarot cards, I Ching, fairy tales, astrology, and getting in touch with our feminine or masculine selves, we are "speaking Jungian."[1] He has become the grand spokesman for New Age thought.

Growing public interest in Oriental religions, shamanism, Navaho sand paintings, alchemy, cultural heritage, and parapsychology can be traced to Jung's depth psychology. Toward the end of his life (he died in 1961), Jung renewed his interest in astrology, parapsychology, and alchemy as ancient methods of psychological transformation. He was criticized for the interest he took in divination, telepathy, clairvoyance, yoga, spiritualism, mediums, flying saucers, séances, fortunetelling, visions, and dreams.

Jung did not approach these subjects as a "believer," but as a psychologist. He wanted to know what these subjects revealed about the mind. As a student of the unconscious, Jung made use of whatever sources there were, no matter how outrageous they might be to other scientists. Jung considered himself a scientist, but he did not abide by tradition or convention.[2] Above all, he was a man in search of his soul.

Jung and Tarot

Tarot has historically been linked with secret societies, esoteric meaning, and aristocratic eccentrics. During the last two decades of the twentieth century, tarot has been studied, written about, discussed, and commercialized—over 100 decks are now available.[3] How did tarot evolve from the veiled mystery of a select few to a lucrative business enterprise and the subject of serious scholarship?

Jung was pivotal in this change. Ironically, he wrote only one sentence about tarot during his long career, but that single sentence laid the foundation for tarot's evolution and popularity. Although he was not part of any esoteric group, his work on archetypes advanced the cause of esoteric study. Jung was a serious scholar. By studying dreams, fantasies, and imagination, he established a rational position from which the irrational could be observed and analyzed rationally.[4]

Jung's theorized that the archetypal unconscious expressed itself through symbols, dreams, fantasies, art, visions, and imagination. His steadfast belief in the scientific method led to a new approach to the nature of tarot symbolism. In his *Integration of Personality* he wrote: "The image series of tarot cards were the descendants of the archetypes of transformation."[5] Brief as it is, this one statement has sparked a mountain of tarot commentary. Open any tarot book written from

1970 to the present day, nearly all will make reference to Jung, archetypes, myth, dreamwork, symbolism, and the work of active imagination. He legitimized tarot. Taking a lead from his pioneering work, practitioners have helped tarot to evolve into a modern tool of transformation and healing, available to all.[6]

Jung and the Shadow

In his book *Archetypes of the Collective Unconscious*, Jung defined "collective unconscious" as that aspect of the unconscious shared by all human beings. It is inherited, a transpersonal residue of evolution, occurring across a variety of social settings. The collective unconscious is not dependent on a single, specific social circumstance for its emergence.*

The components of the collective unconscious are called archetypes, sometimes referred to as patterns of behavior. Archetypes are an essential part of our awareness, capable of illuminating our unconscious behavior—if we allow them. They represent the positive and negative qualities within us. Archetypes form the basis of religion, myth, legend, and fairy tales. They are defined by the culture from which they arise, while their concepts are universal.

The central archetype is the "Self"—the unifying force at the core of our personality pushing us towards wholeness. Jung's other archetypes include the "anima," the feminine principle of caring, responsiveness, and relationships; and the "animus," the masculine character of autonomy, separation, hierarchy, and principle. In Jung's theory, it is essential for women to acknowledge their masculine qualities (animus) and men must recognize their feminine traits (anima) to be whole.[7]

We are aware of heroes, villains, wicked stepmothers, beautiful princesses, vamps, and vampires in every folk tradition throughout the world. For instance, the Mother archetype has existed in all cultures throughout history. She is the feminine principle of creation whether we

---

* This is not a comprehensive look at the theories of C. G. Jung. Volumes have been written by him and about him. The basic information here is intended as a framework to view tarot less as a fortunetelling device and more as a tool of introspection and healing.

call her Sophia, Mary, or Isis. Archetypes, embodied in figures like the Mother, are universal and immediately recognized deep within us. We respond to these universal symbols because they mirror aspects of ourselves.

Of all of these, Jung believed the most powerful archetype to be the Shadow. The Shadow contains the darker aspects of our character that have remained undeveloped because they have not been given expression. Jung suggested these undeveloped feelings, ideas, and desires were animal instincts passed along in evolution and representing the negative sides of our psyches. If neglected, our Shadow will rule us. So powerful is the Shadow, Jung wrote, that if it is not attended to (i.e., made conscious), it will appear in the world around us as our fate.[8]

The Collective vs. Personal Shadow

Jung divided the darker aspects of our personality into two types: the collective shadow and the personal shadow. The collective shadow is made of negative traits held by races of people or countries as a whole, projected onto a minority group or nation. Hitler's soldiers exterminating millions of Jews during World War II, or Protestants and Catholics killing one another in Northern Ireland, offer examples of the collective shadow at work in the world.

The study of the collective shadow and its place in human history could fill several libraries. However, the exclusive focus of *Tarot Shadow Work* is the personal shadow. This manifestation of the shadow contains parts of an individual's psyche that have been forbidden or shamed, depending on cultural and parental conditioning. For example, having many children may be valued in one family, while a successful career is considered more important in another. In the family where children are valued, a woman seeking a career may feel shame and sabotage her own efforts for the sake of her perceived role as parent. In the career-oriented family, a woman with many children may feel shame for failing to establish a career.

Jung once told a friend that he would rather be whole than wholly good. The personal shadow blocks the creative, compassionate aspects of our personalities. When we are young, we are strengthened by resisting undesirable behavior. Later in life, this resistance can develop into a "cut-off" personality trait that stops us from fulfilling our potential.

Me and My Shadow

Throughout this book, "shadow" is defined as unresolved inner conflicts and unexpressed emotions. It refers to those archetypal images which are intuitively recognizable as a troubling part of us: saboteur, martyr, victim, addict, sadist, masochist, or tyrant. The shadow is also present in those latent talents and positive impulses which were discouraged or even banished from our lives at some time on our life path: artistic, musical, athletic, creative talents which have never been realized. Any ability we have not developed, or one that has gone unexpressed for whatever reason, is part of the personal shadow: the lost parts of ourselves. *Tarot Shadow Work* will help readers recover those lost parts.

The Shadow in Daily Life

The stranger called shadow is us and yet apart from us. It is absent from our conscious self-image so that when it does appear, it seems to erupt out of nowhere. It can manifest in a range of behaviors, from blurting out off-color jokes to abusing others or ourselves in life-threatening ways. When you find yourself asking, "What in the world made me do (or say) that?" your shadow is showing. For instance, when a health conscious woman secretly binges on ice cream, her shadow is asserting itself.

The mask we know and show to the world keeps the shadow hidden. The deeper, more unconscious the shadow, the more we experience it as alien to us. We cannot face it in ourselves or tolerate it in another. If you wish to catch a glimpse of your shadow, think of a person you do not like. Describe the qualities in that person that bother you. The characteristics you list are part of your own shadow.

Seeing the traits you dislike in someone else, but not yourself, is called "projection" (more on this theme can be found in chapter 5). Jung suggested we could find the shadow in our slips of the tongue ("What did you mean to say?"), humor (do you laugh at racial, cultural, or sexual jokes?), dreams, daydreams, and fantasies (have you plotted to murder your mother-in-law or boss lately?).

Concrete examples of the shadow include:

* self-destructive behaviors such as addiction and eating disorders
* depression, anxiety disorders, psychosomatic guilt, and shame
* destructive behaviors towards others-verbal, physical and/or sexual abuse
* stealing, lying, marital affairs, envy, blaming, and betrayal[9]

The shadow introduces us to the "other," our "evil twin" or doppelgänger as found in literature. It brings crisis and pain and feels as though it were a separate entity that cannot be tamed or controlled. This beastly shadow shakes us out of our complacency and we are left feeling shamed, disgusted, or outraged at ourselves. We shake our heads and say, "What ever possessed me to _____?!"

The more we fight to suppress and ignore our shadow, the more it controls us. Jung stated that suppression of the shadow was akin to beheading for a headache.[10] He wrote, "if an inferiority is conscious, one always has the chance to correct it . . . but if it is repressed and isolated from consciousness, it never gets corrected."[11]

Symbols and Symbolic Gestures

A symbol (from the Greek συμβολον, "symbolon," meaning "thrown together") expresses something indescribable in ordinary speech and language.[12] It is at once recognizable and understood by an individual or group of people, yet cannot entirely be explained with words. The pentagram, Star of David, and crucifix are examples. Symbols may be sacred or profane, comedic or inspirational, but they share one common trait—they communicate meaning louder than words ever could.

In a sense, symbols are the chosen language of the deeper mind. They tap information stored in our unconscious which has been captured in pictures and images. Dreams, art, and all creative activity open a pathway from the conscious, everyday mind to the unconscious, deeper self.

Often, we ask ourselves what our dreams are trying to tell us. By using the symbolic art of tarot and building a shadow altar, the question can be reversed: What messages are you consciously trying to convey to your deeper, unconscious self? When your logical self is in communication with your intuitive self through symbolic gesture, great change can occur. The symbolic gestures, or rituals, in this book will help you open a dialogue between your conscious mind and your wise, inner self.* Rituals and creating sacred space are examined in chapter 2, "For Brave Souls Only."

Tarot Symbolism

Many theories exist about the origin of the tarot (refer to the recommended reading list in Appendix C for a survey of works). No matter what theory you choose, from Gypsy fortunetelling devices to pastime of the Renaissance rich and famous, one thing is clear—the tarot is laden with instantly recognizable symbolism. The tarot is so exceptionally filled with symbolism, in fact, that it has elements in common with practically every other symbol system in existence: the I Ching, Kabbala, astrology, and many more.[13]

Every tarot card conveys information through its activity, color, scene, the people depicted, or their attitude. Reading the symbols in tarot cards can affect our perceptions and activate our inner selves, thanks to their simplicity and directness of communication. The art of tarot highlights forces and circumstances that have been active in our lives at one time or another. When we see a tarot card that conveys sadness, we say, "Yes, I know the feeling." We may not be able to clearly articulate the experience, but we understand the artwork of tarot intuitively. The universal symbols produce a type of knowing that is not always logical, but always deeply understood. The artist Susan Hill calls this type of understanding "the wisdom that knows without knowing how it knows."[14]

---

* The terms "higher and inner self" are used interchangeably in this book to denote the change that occurs when we travel beyond the limitations of everyday consciousness. This change produces a wiser, creative, healing vision of ourselves and the world.

Approach tarot as the picture book of your life story. The "art" of a tarot reading lies within the symbols of the cards. The best tarot work comes from the heart, not the intellect. Your heart will respond to the pictures. You "read" a card by comparing its symbols to events in your own life; does the card remind you of a situation, relationship, or method of communicating? You can learn many things about yourself by attending to the universal symbolism of tarot on a regular basis. Approach tarot with heart, soul, and feeling. Your mind will follow.

Interpretation of the tarot symbols is in the eye of the beholder. Your own life experience will shape your reactions to the cards. Does the Tower card (16) represent the tower of destruction or the stroke of liberation? Is the Sun (19) representative of the light needed for nourishment and life, or does it mean the scorching heat that lays waste to a desert? The meaning will depend on your frame of reference, your state of mind, and what you are open to perceiving within the cards.

Tarot Shadow Work is not intended to be a basic tarot book, but rather a workbook using tarot symbols. The art of tarot is used in conjunction with self-help techniques to unlock the unconscious and promote healing.

The Shadow in Tarot

Every card has a shadow side rarely mentioned in conventional tarot books. The shadow is generally associated with the Devil card (15), or with the Tower. You get a peek at the shadow when a card appears upside-down in a reading. This book provides an innovative view of reversed cards: the twenty-two cards of the major arcana—the Fool through the World—are depicted here as the dual nature of life (please refer to Appendix A for the shadow meanings of the cards).

Every negative situation is an opportunity to grow and learn, while every positive situation has the potential to spin out of control. For example, the Tower (16) is generally viewed as a negative: destruction, the breakdown of the status quo, holding on to rigid ideas. Yet the Tower can mean the stroke of liberation needed to set a person free from old, restrictive habits or a destructive past. The World (21) is rarely assigned a negative interpretation: the world is your oyster . . . you have many wondrous options . . . you have "arrived." Having many options may be the problem—you have so many options you become frozen, unable to move or decide. When we fear a seemingly "good" thing, our shadow is trying to talk to us.

Any tarot card that evokes strong feelings from you (positive or negative) can represent an unacknowledged aspect of yourself, a lost part of you. Your feelings let you know there is some unfinished business that needs attention. It may be buried deep within you. What are you holding back? What don't you want to see? Anything that prevents you from realizing your full potential is part of the shadow and can be accessed through tarot.

Yin and Yang

Tarot Shadow Work will help you come to terms with the duality of life. Think of the ancient symbol yin/yang. Each teardrop shape begins alongside the fullness of its opposite. As it reaches perfection, its opposite begins again. The sphere is always beginning and ending. To practice lightside/darkside thinking is to practice holding opposites. It means the end of a naïve "all good" view or a cynical "all bad" view of life. Life is no longer a series of yes or no, either-or, all or nothing questions. A gray, neutral area is born where yes and no, all and nothing exist together. This gives us the capacity to tolerate ambiguity and uncertainty. We realize that we are light and dark, and life starts to make sense. When we accept our dual natures, we stop sabotaging our own efforts and learn to be compassionate with ourselves and others.

Shadow Work

The efforts to uncover and understand the shadow are called shadow work. The shadow cannot be eliminated and shadow work is not about fault-finding and blame. The only requirement for doing shadow work is the desire to be honest with yourself.

The question is never, "How can I get rid of this?" but rather, "Where is my shadow now and why might this be happening?" Shadow work does not concern itself with getting rid of anything. It is about fully accepting all aspects of your humanity and changing what is no longer useful with forgiveness and compassion.

Shadow work takes courage because it asks you to fully experience your "demons." When you actively align yourself with your opposite, you will have rediscovered your shadow. By deliberately contacting your shadow and taking hold of your opposites, you become aware. Awareness leads to the power of personal choice and personal choice leads to freedom.

The tricky part of shadow work lies in giving up attempts to control the behaviors you don't like. Shadow work requires that you relax and stop fighting—do not try to slay the shadow! Efforts at controlling and fighting with yourself only allow your shadow to become more powerful. It is in letting go that one finds power. By grasping your opposites and fully acknowledging them, you discover the great irony of life: the act of admitting powerlessness leads to finding power.

This is not the same as an excuse: "Well, if I can't do anything about my shadow behaviors, I'll just continue with _____." We are responsible for our choices and engaging in shadow work is a choice. By taking responsibility for our life, we are now in a position to change the direction of it. In the act of letting go, power and the freedom of choice return.

We can change ourselves with a sense of self-love, forgiveness, and compassion, not self-hatred, condemnation, and shame. When we give the shadow equal time, we eventually extend ourselves, and our responsibility, to all parts of our psyche. Reclaiming the shadow releases tremendous amounts of creative energy and frees us to make choices once again. The rift between us and our shadow becomes whole and healed.

The Challenges and Gifts of Shadow Work

The consequences of ignoring the shadow are high; you may continue to feel anxious, unworthy, out of balance, or shamed. Full potential cannot be realized in these states. Isolation and depression reign, and beauty is lost. Looking into the darkness and being aware of shadow is a complex task, shrouded in mystery. The direction is not clear and it does not lie straight ahead. When you begin this journey, you are asked to trust the process and walk an unknown path. The key to freedom can seem difficult to find. Do gifts really hide in the dark?

When aggression is exiled into shadow, so are leadership skills. When fear of failure hides in the shadow, untapped talents and abilities remain dormant. By plunging into the dark to meet the shadow, the gifts will emerge as well. Accepting aggression uncovers a leader. Facing fear of failure allows talents to surface. There are surprising treasures found in the dark.

Healing

Healing means being all we can be with the challenges and gifts we have. It may or may not involve curing symptoms, but it always entails understanding the meaning of those symptoms. True healing is not the absence of disease, but the presence of insight. What story is being told by our behaviors, symptoms, and illnesses?

Part of the healing process is realizing that every human being contains both darkness and light. The person in pain has an opportunity to understand that others are souls in pain, too. Healing allows us to forgive ourselves through understanding the paradox of life. When we can forgive ourselves for making mistakes, we are able to extend that forgiveness to others with compassion. And compassion heals the world, one soul at a time.

In the Shadow of the Star

In traditional tarot definitions, the Star (17) means everlasting hope. Avoid negativity, concentrate on the positive. The "shadow of the Star" tells us to look closely at the negativity for it is trying to tell us something important about the choices we are making.

Hope, no matter what, can lead to false hope, fantasy, and wishful thinking, like the proverbial ostrich who buries its head in the sand. The nature of shadow is to hide, to remain outside of conscious awareness. The first task of shadow work is to break through fantasy, wishful thinking and denial of the shadow. When we find its hiding place, healing can begin.

In this book, you will learn how to catch a glimpse of the shadow when it appears and to sharpen your senses to it when it erupts. You will learn how to coax the shadow out. This slow process of bringing the shadow to consciousness, forgetting it, and recognizing it again is the nature of shadow work.[15] Eventually, you will learn how to create an ongoing, conscious relationship with your shadow, thereby reducing its power to unconsciously sabotage you.

The light of the stars guides navigators in the night. It can tell us where we are in the dark. The light appears not as the false shine of fantasy and wishful thinking, but as an emanation from the deep source of truth. When we are unknowingly in the Star's shadow, we are standing in the way of our own light. We have lost where we are. Only by understanding our position and our relationship with the shadow can we find our way in the dark.

What Shadow Work Can—and Cannot—Do

I created this method of tarot shadow work as a result of my own losses. It is a concrete way to ease emotional pain, and to realize compassion through the understanding that most of us are souls in pain.

"A house divided against itself cannot stand." By believing parts of ourselves to be "bad," we cannot realize our full potential. We will be fragmented and separated off from ourselves. The "good," qualities we associate with "I, me, and myself" will be at war with the "bad," qualities we associate with "not me." Unresolved conflicts and unexpressed emotions (the shadow) divide us against ourselves. If left unattended, the "house," our sense of self, is structurally weakened and can be easily toppled.

Shadow work asks you to toil on all levels—spiritual, emotional, psychological, and mental. It is the combined effort that produces results. The goal of shadow work is integration, not rejection, of the shadow. Understanding and accepting the shadow will give you wisdom, choice, freedom, power, compassion, and hope.

You can cast spells and recite chants for a better career, but you also need to hit the pavement and complete job applications if you want to find new employment. Incantations and rituals for protection of the home lose potency if you don't lock the front door. The old saying is pray for a better garden, but buy a better hoe.

Shadow work provides you with the right tools for healing, growth, and transformation, but the magic is not in this book—the magic will come from a sincere desire to exercise your power of choice, take action on your own behalf, and allow change to occur.

How to Use *Tarot Shadow Work*

It is helpful to view the workbook as a journey of discovery and not a destination. It is a process rather than a timetable. Go slowly, take your time. It took you a lifetime to be the person you are. It will take time to unravel your life story and reveal the secrets of the you yet to be. Care for yourself during the process of shadow work. Take breaks and play. Celebrate your courage. Revel in the unique person you are, right now, today.

A book is useful only if it is useful to you. Each chapter builds upon itself and is best understood if taken in order. No prior knowledge of tarot is required. Appendix A describes the shadow meanings of the cards. The recommended reading list in Appendix C suggests books for more information on tarot and other topics related to the book. The cards designed and drawn by Robin Wood appear here, but choose any deck that appeals to you. The tarot spreads found throughout the workbook (chapters 3, 4, 6, and 8) may be photocopied for repeated use over time.

Chapter 2, "Descent Into Darkness," gives you the preparation for doing shadow work, including creating sacred space, casting a circle of protection, and building your shadow altar. The Dark Goddess is encountered. You can examine whether or not professional help is indicated by your condition in a section called "How Sad Is Sad?" Shadow work is often painful, and usually brings past hurts to light. It takes courage to meet the shadow. Sometimes, help is needed. You are not alone and help is available. In Appendix B you will find national support groups, organizations, on-line resources and toll-free phone numbers to help you answer life's tough questions.

In chapter 3, "The Darkest Hour" the real shadow work begins. The basic tarot layout, the Star of Discovery, is presented and techniques of journaling and meditation are explained in detail. More methods of shadow work are introduced, such as story writing, poetry, music, art, songwriting, and dance. The methods you choose are up to you. They serve as suggestions to enhance the communication between you and your unconscious.

Chapter 4, "In the Shadow of the Star," explores your personal shadow in depth, with a tarot layout called the Star of Recovery. You are not yet looking for answers at this point, but allowing information to be absorbed. Shadow play offers a creative method for recovering the lost parts of you.

Part II (chapters 5 through 8) starts the process of acceptance, healing, integration, and change.

Chapter 5, "Your Shadow's Power," explores common defense mechanisms. You will hear your shadow speak in a tarot dialogue game. Shadow dreamwork will allow you to enter the mysterious world of your dreams.

In chapter 6, "Embracing Your Shadow," you begin the process of self-acceptance and discovery of the light within. You learn how to contact your own healing potential. The archetype of the Wounded Healer is explored. The Star of Illumination tarot spread identifies areas that need to be healed. You'll also learn how to create realistic goals for change.

Chapter 7, "Compassion—The Inner Light," explores forgiveness of others through compassion. Forgiveness does not mean accepting hurtful behavior, but it does involve letting go of the past through the power of personal choice. Creative visualization techniques help you release old wounds and move on. A Mourning Rite allows for the closure of a painful past; and you can "Wish Upon A Star" for outward expression of the inner light.

The possible future is explored in chapter 8, "The Star of Hope." One of the exercises from the beginning of your journey will be repeated so you can see your progress. Is it time to rebuild your shadow altar?

Because of contact with the inner healer, you'll be able to create a plan for change based on the power of personal choice. Shadow work is a continual, ongoing process of discovery and exploration.

The epilogue offers ideas for future shadow work with tarot.

A Note About Rituals and Tarot Cards

The purpose of rituals is to help us focus on the issue or task at hand. People have discovered over the years that certain actions help them focus on the tarot cards. Some of the most common actions (rituals) are:

* storing the cards in silk or a pine box
* cleaning the cards with repeated shuffling, sea salt, moonlight, crystals, or clary sage
* never letting anyone else touch the cards
* facing north, facing east, facing west when working with the cards; shuffling to the right, shuffling to the left
* lighting candles, burning incense

Opinions vary on the many things you can do with tarot cards. Rituals are personal. You will not, at any time in these pages, be told how to shuffle, deal, clean, or store your cards. That aspect of your tarot experiences is up to you.

If you like rituals and they help you focus on working with the cards, use them. No ritual you perform is sacred unless it is sacred to you. If you develop a habit and the habit helps you focus, use it. Its value is that it helps you to better read the cards. The most powerful rituals are invented by you. Use whatever ritual feels right when working with the cards, or us no ritual at all. You should never do something just because a book tells you to do it. Be aware of why you do what you do. Start exercising your power of choice. Treat the cards the way you treat anything else of value. Tarot can be a powerful tool for transformation and growth, but the "magic" does not come from the cards; the magic comes from you.

Spiritual Systems

Tarot Shadow Work does not ascribe to one spiritual system, although it covers general spiritual work. Chapter 2 describes a method of encountering the Dark Crone Goddess, but use whatever deity works for you: Goddess, God, angel, Spirit Guide, the Christ Light, Allah, Buddha, etc. —this does not represent an inclusive list of possible deities!

If you practice a certain religion, use it here by substituting the name of your deity in place of the one selected. If you are searching for a spiritual base, this workbook can help you find it.

Endnotes

1. Pascal, Eugene. *Jung to Live By.* (New York, Warner Books, Inc., 1992), pp. 3–5

2. Hall, Calvin S. and Vernon J. Nordby. *A Primer of Jungian Psychology.* (New York, New American Library, A Mentor Book, 1973), p. 25

3. Greer, Mary K. *Tarot Constellations.* (North Hollywood, California, Newcastle Publishing, 1987), p. 201

4. Nichols, Sally. *Jung and Tarot.* (York Beach, Maine, Samuel Weiser, Inc., 1980), p. XIV

5. Giles, Cynthia. *Tarot: History, Mystery and Lore.* (New York, Simon and Schuster, 1992), p. 58

6. Ibid., p. 60

7. Echols, Signe, et al. *Spiritual Tarot.* (New York, Avon Books, 1996), p. 9

8. Jung, C. G., *The Collected Works of CG Jung.* R. F. C. Hull, translator. Bollingen Series XX. (New Jersey, Princeton University Press, 1953)

9. Zweig, Connie, Ph.D. and Steve Wolf, Ph.D. *Romancing the Shadow.* (New York, Ballantine Books, 1997), p. 4

10. Berube, Margery S., editor. *The American Heritage Dictionary,* Second College Edition. (Boston, Houghton Mifflin Company, 1985) p. 1230

11. *Religion: West and East.* Vol. 11, paragraph 131 (passage found in *Jung to Live By,* p. 126)

12. Pascal, op. cit., p. 93

13. Giles, op. cit., p. 65

14. "Isabella: Books and Tools for Reawakening the Spirit" (catalog, 1998), vol. 2, p. 2

15. Zweig, op. cit., pp. 8–9

16. Ibid., p. 9

17. Ibid., p. 10

18. Ibid., p. 5

19. Ibid., p. 5

Chapter 2

DESCENT INTO DARKNESS

*A ship is safe in harbor, but that is
not what a ship is for.*
Thomas Aquinas

For Brave Souls Only

IN THIS CHAPTER YOU WILL LEARN HOW ATTITUDES CAN HURT OR HEAL, as well as examining the purpose of pain in your life. It takes courage to face parts of yourself you would rather not know, and it's unwise to face the pain alone. You must ask yourself, "How sad is sad? When is the sadness more than I can handle without help from others?" Guidelines are provided to help you decide if professional counseling should be sought.

Good preparation for shadow work is a must. Being prepared means knowing how to ground and center, cast a circle of protection, create sacred space, and meet the Dark Goddess. In these exercises, always know that you are safe and can leave at any time.

Shadow work is best performed in a nonjudgmental, neutral frame of mind. In this chapter you will practice meditation and make your first journal entries. Read all of this chapter, then go back to the beginning and start doing the exercises. Think of *Tarot Shadow Work* as a verb: its value is in the action you take. No amount of reading can substitute for the action you take on your own behalf.

When you act, you start the process of change by exercising your power of choice. Choice gives birth to freedom and healing occurs.

Attitudes Can Hurt or Heal

Our emotional and physical well-being is closely related to our attitudes about ourselves and life. When we feel good about ourselves we allow good things to happen in our lives. When we don't love ourselves, we allow an opening for negative experiences to come our way. An optimist will see the light at the end of the tunnel. A pessimist will view the light as another train coming to mow her down; same light, different attitude.

The mind is powerful. What you think about affects how you feel and creates experiences which correspond to those feelings. When you believe something to be true, your experiences validate your beliefs. Your attitudes and opinions attract things to you like a magnet. If you feel you are not worthy of love, you will find yourself in unloving situations; if you are loving towards yourself, love will come your way.

Any person or situation in our lives can be viewed either as a challenge or a gift. We have the power to change our attitudes and beliefs whenever we honor our own spiritual values and realize we are worthy of love. One way to affirm ourselves in this way is to examine our attitudes, feelings, and beliefs, changing whatever is no longer useful by exercising the power of choice. We can learn and grow from our experiences, or we can stay locked in the shadows of blame and shame. We can learn compassion for those who suffer just as we do, or our attitudes can turn us into mental cripples. We are the authors and architects of our own lives; how we choose to construct this life is our choice and ours alone.

The Purpose of Pain

Whether physical or emotional, pain is a neutral sign that directs us to a specific issue. Pain grabs us and shouts, "Hey, pay attention to me! I'm trying to tell you something." It serves a purpose and should not be avoided. Suffering in one's life doesn't mean that you are working through bad karma or divine retribution, as some would explain it. Instead, such hardship is a natural part of life, allowing us to flex our spiritual muscles: "No pain, no gain," the old saying goes.

When we spend our lives running away from pain, we end up unable to feel anything, bereft of the happiness and joy we are capable of. Shadow work asks us to hold the tension of opposites and challenges us to grow. And, even when it is properly directed, such growth carries with it a sense of pain—except now the pain has a purpose. It carries the promise of spiritual breakthrough and fulfillment. Once the pain has been experienced, we can move to a place of inner wisdom, peace, and balance.

When the meaning of pain becomes clear, we can face anything. If we sit tight and endure the tension of opposites by quieting our minds, we are able to soar to a higher vantage point. We gain a larger perspective; what appeared to be catastrophic can now be outgrown.

How Sad Is Sad?

Shadow work often uncovers painful, unresolved conflicts and emotions from the past. How bad do we have to feel before outside help should be sought? There are moments in all our lives when we could benefit from professional help.

Countless factors operate in our lives that can interfere with our ability to cope: big decisions, risks, divorce, death, a move, serious illness, loss of job, domestic violence. Even unexpected success can make us feel insecure and more vulnerable to the stresses of everyday life.

When you find yourself concentrating on your inadequacies and suffer the tortures of self-doubt, you should consider getting help. When you arrive at a point of unhappiness enough to want help, it is time to actively seek it.

The wrong questions to ask yourself are about being neurotic or crazy. Instead, ask yourself if you could use some help right now. Don't be afraid to ask for help. Reaching out is a sign of strength and exercises your power of choice.

In holding opposites, alternative and traditional therapies can complement and enhance one another. Professional help need not be viewed as an either/or choice. Tarot shadow work and traditional forms of therapy do not cancel each other out. Rather, therapy provides a valuable adjunct to the work you are doing here with tarot, in your own personal practices. Each carries its own gift of insight and each is valuable.

The average person has the capacity to live through emotionally upsetting situations and bounce back once they are over. It is important to recognize that occasional bouts of anxiety or tension are normal. While it may be unpleasant or painful, such anxiety isn't cause for alarm. So how can you know it is time to seek outside help?

Ask yourself the following questions:[1]

* Has my personality changed? Do people tell me I'm not myself lately?

* Am I having trouble coping with daily activities and everyday problems?

* Am I having strange thoughts or grandiose ideas? Do my ideas scare me?

* Has my anxiety level increased? Am I less able to tolerate change?

* Have I felt depressed or apathetic for a long period of time?

* Has there been marked changes in my eating or sleeping patterns? (increased or decreased)

* Have I had thoughts of or talked about suicide? Have I devised a plan?

* Do I seem to be on a roller coaster of extreme highs and lows?

* Has my use of alcohol or drugs increased? Do I become defensive when someone mentions my use? Do I need alcohol or drugs to get my day started or to face stressful situations? Am I having financial trouble because of my alcohol or drug use? Do I feel a need to hide my use?

* Has my anger level increased? Do I have thoughts of hurting others or injuring myself? Do I hit, slap, throw, or break things in an angry outburst?

If you answered "yes" to any of these questions, outside assistance should be sought. It may be useful to think of professional counseling as a service that specializes in helping people work out their problems. Your primary health care provider can help you decide if there is an underlying medical condition that needs professional attention.

Go to a spiritual advisor of choice, or call your local branch of the Mental Health Association. Many communities now have holistic health centers.

Don't forget your workplace: some employers are recognizing the toll that stress takes on their workers. They are becoming more receptive to offering group exercise, employee assistance plans, and hearing suggestions for improvement in the workplace. Making suggestions for improving the quality of your work environment will result in an increased sense of control over the stress in your professional life (see Appendix B for more information on resources available to you).

Solving problems takes time, work, and energy. Go slowly, but always exercise your power of choice.

The Promise of Shadow Work

In this war between the opposites there is but one battleground—the human heart. The heart is tender and easily broken. It is also the strong gateway to healing. While shadow work is painful, and is certainly not a game, take heart that you can persevere through this journey of healing. Take good care of yourself during this time. Celebrate your courage.

Working slowly is essential. You are trying to heal old wounds, not create new ones. Do not look for rapid change. In our fast-paced, flick-of-the-switch culture, it is tempting to seek immediate results. You have probably been responding to life in a set pattern for years: it will take time to change your responses.

Your goal in shadow work is to observe the shadow, to witness the shadow's pattern through self-observation and awareness. Be with the shadow but don't try to slay it. Later you will meet the shadow and feel a greater choice. You will not be compelled to obey. You can choose to reject its message rather than act it out. You will be freed of the shadow's power. What once had been an enemy is now an ally.

As you continue to bring the shadow into the light, you will regain your rightful place as the author of your own life. The shadow will be but one character in your life story. You will be able to make self-affirming, conscious decisions for the benefit of the whole process. The shadow will return to its proper place in a cast of many characters within your life, not the central figure. Within the context of this ensemble cast, the shadow can be heard and honored in an appropriate way through creative expression. A new chapter in your life will be written.

Preparation for Shadow Work

Shadow work must be practiced in an atmosphere of safety. Know you can stop and leave at any time. You need to be grounded and protected during this potentially painful work. Grounding allows you to develop the capacity for self-observation. You are tuning in to the voice of self.

When you can witness your thoughts, feelings, and sensations with some detachment, you can experience them fully without allowing them to take over. A temporary emotion will not become your whole life. "I am sad" will become "I feel sadness, but I know it will pass" within your grounded circle of protection.

Read all the suggestions given before proceeding to do any exercises. Pick and choose. If something you read doesn't "feel" right, don't do it. If a section stimulates your own ideas, go with your creativity. The more personal you make shadow work, the more meaningful (and beneficial) it will be to you.

Creating Sacred Space— Building Your Shadow Altar

It is important to be spiritually centered while doing shadow work. Your intuitive, creative side—the Higher Self—is fed by images. Let go of any notion that spirituality and sensuality don't mix. Your shadow altar should provide a sensory experience, for it is this part of you that communicates with the unconscious.

The small rituals you create for yourself are good for the soul. Burning incense, lighting candles, listening to chants, holding a crystal, dancing, or drumming—all these actions reinforce spiritual growth. No ritual is sacred unless it is sacred to you. Use your own spiritual system while creating your shadow altar. The following ideas are only suggestions to get you started.

Anything you do must have meaning for you. The goal of building a shadow altar is to help you focus on the important spiritual work you are about to undertake. Your unconscious speaks to you in art, images, dreams, and fantasies. Make your altar a creative, visual experience.

Building an altar literally involves putting spirituality into physical form; it is *not* like decorating. Altars provide important reminders of what we sometimes forget in the day-to-day rush of living: to reflect, to live with purpose, to connect to our personal sense of the divine. A shadow altar will connect you with your deepest, innermost self. You will hear the still, small voice within that gives you messages about your personal growth and progress on earth. Your shadow altar will help you work through emotional pain. It will assist you to move through your feelings until they are no longer raw, yet fully acknowledged.

Everything about your altar is ultimately personal and will reflect your individuality, your life, your experiences, your pain, your shadow. Know that when you build an altar, you are connecting with an ancient rite.

Choosing a room

Available space, convenience, and privacy are important factors to consider when choosing your sacred space. It can be a corner of your bedroom, a nook under the stairs, a window ledge, a shelf in your bathroom—anywhere there is space. Ideally, it needs to be large enough to accommodate a six-card tarot layout. You decide the privacy issue. Does it need to be portable, easily set up and taken down? Are you uncomfortable with the idea of people gazing at your shadow altar? Choose your sacred space accordingly.

Direction

North is the ideal direction for shadow work because it is the direction of the Goddess, and is associated with winter, the time of introspection. During winter we burrow deep and come back up with true knowledge and wisdom. Face your altar north to begin the journey of self-discovery.

There are good reasons to use other directions: west, for example, connects you with water and your intuitive self. If you have a sincere desire to do shadow work, it doesn't matter which direction your altar faces. Others will disagree, but if space is at a premium, the Goddess is, above all, practical. Set your shadow altar up in the space you have available.

Color

Black is the color of shadows, night, death (of the old), the Underworld, and mystery. Black belongs to Crone wisdom. Purple is the color of profound healing, deep wisdom, protection, and your spiritual self. White is associated with purity, initiation, spiritual knowledge, light, hope, and psychic protection. It is an all-purpose color. Dark blue or gray can symbolize confusion, depression, or illness. True blue is a healing color and rose signifies universal love. Brown is the color of the earth, home, and animal healing or protection.

Candles and cloths made of natural fabrics add visual interest and atmosphere to your altar. The colors you choose for them need to be aligned with shadow work. You may wish to change the color of your altar as you progress. Red can symbolize anger or sexuality, green your career or finances. If you are in school, yellow, the color of intellectual pursuits, is appropriate. Start with black or purple. As the mystery unfolds, allow your intuition to guide you in choosing color.

Incense, oils, and flowers

Orchids are associated with the dark moon and the Crone. Vanilla is a by-product of the orchid. Lilies symbolize death and rebirth. Night-blooming flowers, such as jasmine, can represent the Crone and her mysteries. Any heavy scent, including opium, neroli, black narcissus, myrrh, and musk, is aligned with shadow work. Sandalwood and frankincense are all-purpose substitutes, especially for protection.

Figurines, objects, and amulets

Selecting objects for your altar is a personal choice. If you feel an object is correct for your altar, it is. Consider using pictures, jewelry, or anything else you hold dear. The most important factor in choosing items for the shadow altar is that it has meaning and symbolism for you. The following suggestions serve only to activate your intuition.

Objects and figurines symbolic of Crone wisdom, mystery, and the Underworld include claws set in silver, ravens, serpents, spiders, owls, and black cats. They can be worn as jewelry or carried in your pocket to remind you of your work as you go about your day-to-day activities.

Stars provide light as we navigate the night. Five-pointed stars, called pentagrams, are sacred to witches and other followers of earth religions. The five points symbolize earth, air, fire, water, and spirit, and its enveloping circle means the endless cycle of life, death, and rebirth. It is associated with the feminine and is powerful for protection.*

Apples have represented knowledge since time began. In Celtic beliefs, the spirit goes to Avalon, or Land of the Apples. They are symbols of the soul. Apples signify death, rebirth, and wisdom.

Stones and crystals

Dark stones and crystals are appropriate for shadow work: smoky quartz, shale, slate, black obsidian. If you are comfortable with black onyx, use it, especially if you have a lot of Capricorn in your natal (birth) horoscope. Onyx can cause depression in some, but it is a potent stone for those aligned to it.

Amethyst is a beautiful crystal and symbolizes wisdom and healing. Rose quartz radiates universal love. It is a good choice for chapters 6 and 7: forgiveness and compassion. It is wise to avoid diamonds during shadow work unless the gem is particularly meaningful to you. Diamonds hold, absorb, magnify, and transmit pain; they retain impressions and are difficult to clear. Positive diamonds transmit pure knowing and spirit, so you decide whether or not to use them.

---

* The pentagram is not related to the Christian Devil because witches do not believe in any devil. This association is an aberration of Christianity and an example of that religion's collective shadow (see chapter 1).

Moonstone is a balancing energy between opposites and is effective for meditating on life's dualities and paradox (life-death, give-take, yes-no). Moonstone stimulates self-awareness and assists in balancing the rational and intuitive self.[2]

Lapis lazuli is an overall healer and it stimulates Crone spirituality. Use lapis in the later phases of shadow work. If you want to contact your anger, especially during the discovery/recovery phase of shadow work (chapters 3 and 4), choose red and orange stones. Amber, tiger's-eye, and carnelian are especially effective when working with fear.

Clear quartz crystal is a good all-purpose stone as it connects with spirit and has a cleansing effect. Any stone you find in nature that speaks to you personally is always a good choice.

Metals

The Crone is associated with aging and wisdom. She has gray, white or silver hair. Silver and platinum symbolize the Crone. Some people are allergic to silver. If you react to silver, or simply prefer gold, please substitute.

Herbs and plants

Willow, oak, moss, cedar, and garlic are appropriate. Cyclamen blossoms remove grief of the heart. Witch hazel is used for protection and mends a broken heart. Mandrake is good for protection but it is expensive. Substitute may apples, apples, or ash root.

Yarrow is used for courage. Mint will call good spirits as will marjoram and rosemary. Motherwort brews a nice tea and is helpful with attuning to feminine wisdom (it also assists with regulation of heavy bleeding during menopause). Apple-flavored tea is an effective brew for getting in touch with Crone wisdom. Add honey, if desired.

Please use caution: Plants such as hemlock, foxglove, and belladonna (nightshade) are toxic to touch and deadly poison. They should be avoided. Foxglove can cause fatal cardiac arrhythmia. Check with an herbologist or health specialist of choice before handling or ingesting plants. Most health food stores selling herbs have in-house experts, or refer to *Cunningham's Encyclopedia of Magical Herbs* (Llewellyn, 2000).

Pictures, jewelry, mementos, and family heirlooms can symbolize situations from your past that arise during the course of shadow work. You will probably change items as your focus changes. Meditate about your shadow altar (more on meditation later in this chapter). You may receive insight concerning what to place there.

This is not an all-inclusive list. If Buddha or the Virgin Mary are sacred to you, honor them. Remember, no ritual you do is sacred unless it is sacred to you. Anything that brings your personal spirituality into physical form has a rightful place on your altar.

Grounding, Centering, and the Circle of Protection

Think of this exercise as learning to stand on solid ground inside yourself. You can quiet your mind, relax your body, settle your emotions, and witness the shadow. Grounding and centering prepares you to meet the shadow with awareness and the capacity to respond effectively. Don't skip this step. If you've had success with other rituals of protection, include them in the exercise.

In the beginning it may take fifteen to twenty minutes to get to this safe place. As you practice, you will find yourself reaching it in three minutes or less. Choose a time when you are free of outside distractions and will not be interrupted, unplug your phone, and do what it takes to be alone.

It can be helpful to record these exercises on tape and play them back when you are ready to ground and center. Relaxing background music, candles, or incense will enhance the effect. Dim the lights in the room, if necessary, to enjoy the glow of the flames or embers.

Sit comfortably before your shadow altar, if possible, or sit comfortably on the floor or in a chair with your arms in your lap. Begin by taking three slow, deep breaths. As you inhale, become aware of any tension or pain you feel in your body. Don't try to change it, but note where it is. As you breathe out, imagine that all this tension or pain is leaving you through the souls of your feet. Continue breathing in a slow, deep way. Allow the air to fill your abdomen. When you exhale, feel the air leave your abdomen and travel to the very top of your lungs. Breathe in, notice tension. Breathe out, feel the tension leave. Deep-breathe in this manner until you feel yourself relax.

Continue breathing in this slow, deep way throughout the remainder of the exercise. Next, as you inhale, bring energy in from the soles of your feet. Allow it to travel through your body and come to a resting place around your heart. On exhalation, feel all your tension and worries leave through the soles of your feet and go into the ground. You have now connected with the strength of Mother Earth. Continue breathing in a slow careful way and feel the Mother's strength.

As you inhale, bring light from above your head down into your heart. Allow it to rest in your heart and fill you with a sense of well-being, health, and love. Notice the color of the light. Is it white? Pink? Gold? Purple? As you exhale, send this light out through your heart and create a circle of light around you. See the circle. Feel the warmth and glow. (If you have difficulty actually seeing the circle, simply say out loud: "I cast this circle of protection around me and feel safe and protected at all times." It will work.)

Continue breathing deeply. On the next inhalation, bring Mother Earth up through your feet and rest her in your heart. Exhale all your worries. When you breathe in again, bring the light above you down through the crown of your head and place it in your heart. Hold your breath for a moment to allow the energy of Mother Earth and the Light of Spirit to mix. Exhale slowly. You are both grounded, with a sense of strength and protection and in Spirit, with a sense of well-being, health, and love.

As you breathe light in, allow it to turn to a beautiful shade of deep purple. When you exhale this purple light, see it envelop you in a sphere. It surrounds you and you are safe. Feel at once protected and profoundly loved. Say out loud: "I charge this circle with only the most perfect energies compatible with my purposes of doing shadow work. By embracing my dark shadows, I am healing and becoming whole. I am gaining wisdom and learning compassion. This is correct and for the good of all, according to free will. Harm none. So must it be."

Stay with this feeling of well-being for a while. Continue to breathe in a slow, deep way. Know you can return to this place of safety and love at any time, in any place. Count slowly backwards from five. As you say each number, feel yourself return to normal consciousness, but with a feeling of relaxation and well-being. You are refreshed, protected, loved, and ready to encounter the Dark Goddess.

The Three Faces of the Goddess

Much has been written about the three faces of the Goddess archetype as Maiden, Mother, and Crone (refer to Appendix C for recommended reading). Shadow work takes the Crone as its divine focus.

The Maiden has many names: Artemis, Diana, Aradia, Macha, and countless others. Regardless of her name, she is connected with youth, first menstruation, puberty, adventures, the wilderness, and animals. She is the Lady of the Hunt and her time is the waxing, or increasing, phase of the moon. Call upon her for any new beginning, especially in relationships or work. She can give you a freer, more independent and confident attitude.

The Mother archetype represents the body as vessel, childbearing, nurturance. She is called Demeter, Isis, Ceres, Freya, Astarte, Ishtar, Cerridwen, and Epona. The Mother provides for and nourishes the earth and her time is during the full moon. She is fertile, creative, menstruating, living in her prime. Call upon her for manifesting your goals, blessings, protection (no one protects like a mother protecting her young!), growing, making choices, childbirth, protection of animals, creativity, and spiritual direction.

The Crone Goddess is the elder wise-woman, Grandmother Spider, acquainted with the night, decay, and death. She encompasses duality and, at once, holds dark and light, life and death, destruction and creation. She is called Hecate, Kali, Dana, Nemesis, Rhiannon, the Banshee, and the Morrigan. The Crone is past her time of bleeding and is the Keeper of the Mysteries at the gateway to the Underworld. She can see the past, present, and future at once and is the Goddess of Prophecy. Her time is at the waning, or decreasing, moon. She tends the cauldron of death and rebirth. Her wisdom is helpful to women of any age. The Crone has the ability to put things in perspective and let you see your current situation against an eternal backdrop. Her special children are elders, widows, people with life-threatening illnesses, and all souls in pain. The Crone offers strength and comfort in the dark. She will not seek or call upon you; you must search for her and learn to trust the darkness. Her gifts are wisdom, transformation, clairvoyance, protection, peaceful endings, and profound spiritual healing.

The Crone is also the Goddess of Retribution and Justice. Call upon her for protection against sexual harassment, domestic violence, and rape. Be certain your request is unselfish and justified. If it's not, you may find yourself being chased by her vengeance. This Goddess, more than any other, believes in equal opportunity. She plays no favorites and does not respond kindly to malicious or frivolous requests. Remember the threefold law when working with any of these Goddesses: Whatever you send out will come back to you three times stronger. Be certain your intent is pure, especially when working with the energy of the Crone.

Call upon Crone power during shadow work. She can assist you in developing your inner guide. She promises communication with your ancestral past and will aid you in contacting your eternal spirit. The Crone will help you see the grand scheme of things and understand the deepest mysteries.

All the Goddess archetypes are positive, but the Crone is often feared. Many books will advise you to stay away from the dark phase of the moon. The Crone is misunderstood. After all, she became the ugly hag with warts on Halloween. We live in a youth-oriented culture with no use for the wisdom of our elders, our televisions are flooded with commercials for "age-defying" make-up, and eternally adolescent female stars prance around the media unopposed. Sadly, older women in the United States are part of a "throwaway society," cast out and relegated to nursing homes. We can't bring ourselves to say the words "death" or "die"; people "pass on," "expire," or are "lost."

I suggest that the Crone offers new ways of exploring possibilities and new ways of interacting with the world. Rather than selecting "acceptable parts" of the Crone to work with, perform shadow work with her entire feminine energy. Instead of fragmenting your attention, cutting yourself off from your nature, recognize that "all of this is me." Shadow work returns you to a state of integration and wholeness that encompasses the totality of your personality.

Encountering the Dark Goddess

Perform this visualization to contact your inner wisdom. Remember, all of this is you. You are safe and protected and can leave at any time. The Dark Goddess/Wise Woman/Crone is the Keeper of the Gate. She holds the key that will unlock the deep mystery of your shadow. It is helpful to tape-record the meditation and play it back when you are ready to meet her. Disconnect the phone so you will not be interrupted. Allow at least twenty minutes for this exercise.

Loosen any tight clothing. Sit or lie comfortably with your eyes closed. Breathe slowly and deeply. As you exhale, feel all the tension and cares of the day leave your body through the soles of your feet. As you inhale, pull in beautiful, deep purple light from above you. Let it fill you with a sense of peace. Allow your attention to withdraw into yourself. Repeat the shadow work affirmation: "By embracing my dark shadows I am healing and becoming whole. I am gaining wisdom and learning compassion."

When you are ready, picture yourself approaching an ancient forest. A path opens up in front of you. You follow it deep into the heart of the forest. It is night with no moon in the sky. Only one star guides your way in the dark.

You come to a bridge where three roads converge. Each road has a sign post. You look closer and see the roads are named "Past," "Present," and "Future." The scents of night-blooming jasmine and vanilla are heavy in the air. You see an old woman on the bridge and ask if you may join her. She motions you towards her. As you approach, you notice her beautiful silver hair. She is dressed in a flowing purple and black robe. Her only adornments are an amethyst crystal and an orchid in her hair. You have never seen anyone like her before. Her eyes are at once sad and kind. Her face is deeply wrinkled, yet more lovely because of it. You sense she has experienced the whole cycle of life—she has known joy and sorrow, birth and death. There's a familiarity about her, as though you have known her before.

You are now close to her on the bridge and feel loved and protected. You spend time with her and ask her to share her wisdom and experience. She takes you deep within yourself where her knowing resides. You continue to talk and ask her questions.

After a while, you know it is time to leave. She gives you a gift nestled inside a purple box. You open the box and thank her for her gift. What has she given you? You tell her you will treasure it always and marvel at her for being there just when you needed her. She reassures you she is accessible to you at any time, if you request her presence.

You turn and make your way back through the forest, returning to your starting point. The heavy scents of the night air start to fade. Take deep breaths and gradually become aware of your own surroundings. Take time to adjust and slowly open your eyes when you are ready.

Write your experience down. Be as detailed as possible. Write everything that comes to mind—do not censor your writing. What did you learn? What was your gift? Why do you suppose she gave it to you? What did she tell you? Were you comforted or afraid of the Crone? Why? Is she someone you want in your life? Will you invite her back? Why or why not? Regardless of your current age, what can you learn from the Dark Goddess? Do you want her knowledge? Why or why not? Let your writing flow without editing it. Read your entry periodically as you progress through shadow work. Jot down your impressions of the Wise Woman as they change.

Why Meditate?

Meditation is an ancient art practiced extensively in Hindu, Taoist, and Buddhist traditions, as well as in more recent interpretations of the Judeo-Christian religions. All cultures practice some form of meditation. When the body undergoes the deep relaxation of the meditative state, the autonomic nervous system responds with a decreased heart rate, lowered blood pressure, decreased respiratory rate and oxygen consumption, and decreased brain wave activity (beta to alpha waves). When practiced regularly, meditation produces a calming sense of control over the emotions.[3]

Besides decreasing stress, meditation allows you to access your inner wisdom and find, or recover, lost parts of yourself. It increases your awareness of the unity of the universe and improves your ability to function in day-to-day reality. Meditation increases stamina, quiets the mind, and promotes an enthusiasm for living. Most of all, meditation can strengthen your spiritual connection.[4]

The Tools of Meditation

The greatest aid to achieving a meditative state is the intention to still the mind. You cannot "force" meditation—you must wait for it to happen.

Visualization is a simple method used to achieve the meditative state where imagery provides the focus for relaxation. Imagery can take you to a peaceful place where you are calm and the mind gradually becomes stilled.

Chanting and sounds made on instruments such as drums, bells, or tambourines can be powerful focal points. A photo, picture, or symbol from your shadow altar may initiate the visual focusing of attention. Chapter 3 explores meditating with the powerful symbols of tarot card artwork.

Peg Streep's book *Altars Made Easy* (HarperCollins, 1997) offers detailed information about meditation tools.

Your Life Is a Busy Place— Dealing with Distractions

In the early stages of learning meditation you may be aware of distractions—the ringing phone, the mental note to pick up light bulbs on your next trip to the store, the hurried glance at the clock to reassure yourself you haven't forgotten your eye exam. Your body may itch, the refrigerator will hum decibels louder than usual. These are simply distractions of the mind. Be aware of them and let them go. You may suddenly remember you must send a birthday card to Great-Aunt Tillie and you need to put air in your tires before you drive another mile. Thoughts will come into your mind. Let them pass through you without hanging on to them. Note the things that distract you and how your mind complains that it has nothing to do and is bored. Treat your mind kindly but firmly, much like a child learning an important skill. Let the distractions go.

Establishing a Meditation Ritual

Choose a regular time and place for meditation. Dawn and dusk are especially tranquil. Meditate in front of, or near, your shadow altar. Light candles, burn incense, repeat the shadow work affirmation. All such actions signal the mind that you want it to cooperate with you and honor your sacred time and space.

Once you are sitting comfortably, change your pattern of breathing. The act of breathing slowly and deeply is a powerful focus for attention. If your mind wanders off, bring it gently back to your breathing.

The Healing Heart Meditation

Choose a time when you will be undisturbed for twenty minutes. Loosen any tight clothing. Disconnect the phone. Light incense and a candle from your shadow altar. Play relaxing, soft music. Tape-record the meditation or have someone read it to you. Begin as with all the exercises in this book—breathe slowly and deeply. Exhale all your concerns and worries of the day. Inhale a feeling of calm and well-being. When you notice yourself becoming more relaxed, focus your attention on the area around your heart. This is the area of your spiritual ideal and it is where all healing takes place.

Breathe out your cares. Breathe in a beautiful rose-pink light. Let it surround your heart and fill you with a sense of well-being. Allow the rose-pink light to expand, fill your body, and radiate all around you. Take your time. Breathe slowly. You feel safe, calm, and loved.

Without expectation, know you are entering sacred space to be with your Higher Self. Be still and at peace. Allow your thoughts to enter and leave without censoring them. Regard them with detachment and, if your mind wanders, bring it back to your rose-colored heart center and your slow, deep breathing. The still, small voice within you only whispers, it never shouts. Listen for communication with your Higher Self.

Come back into your body calmly and deliberately. Become aware of your surroundings, the placement of your feet and your contact with the ground. Open your eyes and gradually return to normal consciousness. Know that the feeling of universal love is available to you again, anytime and anywhere. It is always surrounding you whether you are aware of it or not. Feel connected to something greater than yourself. Above all, know you are loved and have always been so. Record your experience in your journal.

Journaling

Your journal is a memoir of your shadow work, a recorded moment in your life. As such, it is a deeply personal diary. View keeping a journal as a process of self-discovery and not an end result, a journey rather than a destination. Journaling, as it is often called, allows you to put into words your innermost thoughts without fear of criticism. A journal is your personal property and it can be kept confidential.

The healing effect from journaling comes from the process of writing your innermost thoughts, feelings, insights, and observances. You can vent rage in a journal without fear of reprisal. You can be sad, silly, humorous, or anything else you want to be. It is your life story and you are the author. Your journal becomes the chronicle of the shadow work process. Whether you share it with anyone else is up to you. As you read previous entries again, you will find your journal to be a record of personal growth, insight, and wisdom.

Many beautiful blank books are available for purchase, but you need not spend a lot of money on your journal. A three-ring notebook or file folder is adequate. The exercises in this book can be written on loose-leaf, college-lined paper and added to your notebook or folder.

Journal entries can be jotted down at odd moments, but you may want to set aside a special time specifically for writing about the shadow. Entries need to be made on a regular basis, particularly in the beginning phases of shadow work. Date each entry. If you wish to go back and add to a certain day, use a different color ink and date that entry, too. You will soon have a record of emerging shadow patterns. (Chapter 3 covers writing about your shadow in detail. Dream work and keeping a dream journal are introduced in chapter 5.)

Once the value of journal keeping has been established, you will find it becomes a trusted daily ritual during which you record your feelings, traumas, pain, joy, triumphs, and insights. For most people, this is therapy enough. For others, journaling can be the key to realization that some therapy or self-help group is appropriate. This is particularly true if issues from the past, such as physical or emotional abuse, are still having an effect on the present.

The journal will help you make important connections between your conscious mind and your unconscious self, where the shadow resides and has its power. You are now ready to meet your shadow.

Endnotes

1. Used by permission of the American Psychiatric Association, 1400 K Street, N.W., Washington, DC 20005, phone: (202) 682-6000. For more information, visit APA Online, www.psych.org, The American Psychiatric Association, "Choosing a Psychiatrist" (Washington, DC, 1993, revised 1997). Keyword: mental health, click "psych online."

2. Stein, Diane. *The Women's Book of Healing* (Minnesota: Llewellyn Publications, 1994), p. 225

3. Krieger, Delores. *The Therapeutic Touch* (New York: Fireside, Prentice Hall Books, 1979), pp. 157–158

4. Keegan, Lynn, Ph.D., RN. *The Nurse as Healer* (New York: Delmar Publishers, 1994), p. 175

Chapter 3

THE DARKEST HOUR

Where is there height without depth, and how
can there be light that throws no shadow?

C. G. Jung

Me and My Shadow

THE FIRST STAGE OF SHADOW WORK, AFTER PREPARATION, IS DISCOVERY. As simple as it seems, you don't know what you don't know. The purpose of this chapter is awareness and the goal is discovery. In the process of discovery, try to be a detached observer of your life. Reserve judgments. Allow information to surface without attaching blame. You are not trying to change anything at this stage. Imagine listening to a friend relate the story of his life. You make objective comments and help your friend. Be with the information and nothing more.

The first tarot card spread is called the Star of Discovery and is followed by meditation and journal exercises. Other activities for shadow work are found at the end of the chapter.

The Purpose of Fear—
What Your Shadow Knows

The purpose of defense mechanisms is to protect us from emotional pain. Anger is really the fear that we might not get what we want in a given situation. Life is change and nothing stays the same. Change is both a fact of life and a cause for distress. We learn fear early. From the moment of birth, we have the need for food, shelter, and love. If for any reason our needs are not met, we know fear. Fear drives us to get what we need in order to survive.

The survival purpose of fear soon begins to permeate all aspects of our lives. We learn there is no endless source of anything. We are taught to live by the fear of loss. We align ourselves with fear: we fear someone will die, we fear we won't have enough money, we fear our significant relationships will dissolve, or happiness won't last, we fear being alone. This is where our fear of, and resistance to, change originates, and where our shadow starts to grow.

The mind generates both positive and negative thoughts. We have a choice in how we wish to think. Think of this example. Two neighbors are outside in their yards when a powerful thunderstorm begins. The sky turns black, illuminated only by bolts of lightning. One neighbor rushes into the house and down to the basement. He cowers in fear because he expects a tornado. The other neighbor also dashes into the house, but he grabs his video camera. He runs outside again and starts filming because he expects a splendid display from Mother Nature. Same storm, different choice: one is aligned to fear, the other is not.

It is your choice how you will perceive an event in your life. In the process of discovering the shadow, an event from your past cannot hurt you today unless you give it the power to hurt you today. Know that you are safe. Today you learn the power of choice; you can choose to look at past events as a detached observer, without fear. The rest of the chapter will teach you how.

Meditation and Tarot

One of the best ways to understand the message in a tarot card is to meditate with it. Use the pictures as a focal point for your meditation (see chapter 2) and attend to whatever thoughts come into your mind. Mentally converse with a card. Ask it about its shadow meaning. Your inner wisdom will whisper to you

Look at the major arcana* cards of your tarot deck, numbers 0–21 (the Fool through the World). Be aware of your initial reactions, without censoring them, for they are most likely to be from your intuitive self. Determine why you like or dislike particular cards. Are you indifferent to others? Why does a card make you feel uneasy, frightened, angry, happy, or sad? Why? Record your thoughts and feelings in the journal. The images that evoke the strongest feelings—both positive and negative—can represent an unacknowledged part of yourself, your shadow. Strong feelings towards a card are usually a tip-off that some inner business needs to be finished. Discovering unfinished business is the essence of shadow work.

Reversed Cards and the 8-11 Difference

Tarot Shadow Work is an application of tarot—one more way to use tarot for personal growth. Because it is not a basic tarot "textbook," it does not deal with the 8-11 and reversed card controversies. Some decks show Strength as 8, Justice as 11. Other decks reverse it—Justice is 8, Strength is 11.

Reversed card meanings in a layout cause an even greater controversy among tarot authors. Much has been written about both subjects. Mary K. Greer explains it beautifully in *Tarot for Your Self* (Newcastle Publishing, 1984). *Choice Centered Tarot* by Gail Fairfield (Samuel Weiser, 1997) clarifies the dilemma with eloquent simplicity.

For the purpose of shadow work, it does not matter whether your deck has Strength or Justice as the number 8 card. The nuance of the card remains the same. If a card appears reversed (upside-down) in one of the star spreads, interpret it as a sign of its importance. In effect, a reversed card says to you, "Hey, look at me. I'm important because I am different." A reversed card draws attention to itself and this is sufficient understanding for shadow work.

---

* Major arcana means "great secrets."

A reversed card can also be operating on a deeply psychological or unconscious level, with its significance not apparent to you. Be patient. Its meaning will become clear as you progress in knowing the Other. Shadow work brings the darkness to light.

Entering and Leaving a Tarot Card

The key to understanding tarot is to allow it to come to life. The sooner you connect a card with a real situation, the sooner you understand its message. If you are feeling confused or undecided and the Moon (18) comes up in a spread, look at the artwork on the Moon and feel the confusion. When you see it again in another layout, you will remember the feeling without memorizing anything. Always look at the card with which you are working. As simple as it seems, many people get stuck memorizing an author's definitions and never personalize tarot or connect visually to the art. No amount of word memorization from Appendix A can replace the artistic symbolism of the picture. Connecting to a card's artwork is the most rapid way to learn tarot or use tarot as a tool for shadow work.

Disconnect the phone and remove all potential distractions from your environment. Hold the card comfortably before you where you can see the picture without straining your eyes. Breathe slowly and deeply to achieve a relaxed state. Concentrate your breathing in the heart area and allow it to fill with rose-pink light on every inhalation. Breathe out all your cares and worries. Repeat your affirmation: "By embracing my dark shadows, I am healing and becoming whole. I am gaining wisdom and learning compassion." Know that you are safe and can leave at any time.

When you feel relaxed, allow the edges of the tarot card to soften. Gaze indirectly at the card until it is slightly out of focus but not blurry. Do not strain your eyes to "force" this to happen. Breathe deeply and allow it to happen in its own time. Be patient.

See the card grow larger in your mind's eye. As it enlarges, you clearly see that the people and things of the card are alive and interacting. You are curious and want to be there. As you step through the border of the card, you become part of the living scene. You are now in the card. What thoughts come into mind as you join the picture? What is around you? What do you see, hear, feel, and smell? Is there anything to taste? What color, mood, and feeling predominates? Is the atmosphere light, heavy, stagnate, or flowing? Is it electrically charged? Do you feel fear? Why might that be so? Are the characters happy, sad, angry, or neutral? What could this tell you about your shadow?

Look around and notice as many details about the surroundings as you can. Tell yourself you are safe and can leave at any time. Say aloud that you will remember the experience without fear when it's time to leave the card. Approach the characters and animals in the card and ask them questions. What is happening? How did they get there? Ask the characters to tell you about themselves. What do they reveal? How do they represent your shadow self? Stay and interact with them until you sense it is time to leave. Thank them for allowing you to be a part of their lives.

Turn around and step back through the picture. You are back in your own surroundings. As you breathe deeply, the card returns to its normal size and the picture on it is once again two-dimensional. Allow your eyes to focus on the card until it is clear. Look at it in focus for a few more moments as you adjust yourself to normal consciousness. Thank your inner wisdom for the opportunity to grow and record the experience in your journal. What did you learn about your shadow?

The Tarot Journal

The tarot journal may be kept as part of your shadow work journal. Each tarot reading is one step in your journey towards wholeness. Keeping a record of your readings over time allows you to monitor your inner development.

If you see some of the cards repeating themselves in your shadow layout, there is a message calling for your attention. A theme in your life, represented by the repetitive card, needs examination. Sometimes the dark symbols of tarot artwork are not immediately clear. By keeping a tarot journal, you can review unclear readings next week or next month. You may be surprised by how much sense the cards make when reviewed at a later time. Always date any tarot journal entry.

Honor all information you receive regardless of whether or not you grasp it today. Adopt an attitude of respectful regard and do not dismiss cards you do not understand. Over time, with patience and meditation, the puzzle pieces will fall into place.

Writing About Your Shadow

When we hold the paradox that the shadow is both stranger and kin to us, we enter into one of the great mysteries of the psyche. The shadow lengthens as day falls and is at its fullest toward the moment of twilight. Writing about your shadow allows you to enter twilight time.

During the course of shadow discovery, imagine yourself to be an undercover observer. You are perfectly disguised while living the life of the Other. Who is the character you become to save your life? Imagine yourself invisible and follow your shadow through the day. How does he behave when people are watching? Observe him when he is alone. What does he think about when he is sleepless at 3:00 A.M.? What secrets are you privy to? What essential part of yourself is covered up by a persona?

Question, observe, and be curious about everything. Accept all you observe and come to know. Be careful not to make judgments or let fear contaminate your words. We always cast a shadow, but how we relate to it depends on whether or not it is known.

Before You Begin

Begin a tarot shadow work session by grounding, centering, casting a circle of protection, and repeating the shadow work affirmation (refer to "Entering and Leaving a Tarot Card" in the preceding pages). If time allows and you wish it, encounter the Dark Goddess and meditate before the shadow altar. At the very least, disconnect the phone and take slow, deep breaths to achieve a state of relaxation. Light candles and burn incense to cue your unconscious that something important is about to happen.

The following journal exercise without the cards is designed to give you a sense of where you are right this moment as you take the first steps of your journey. Your entry will be compared to a similar exercise at the end of the book. Think of it as a compass or gauge of your inner growth. When you have breathed deeply and feel relaxed, answer these questions in your journal: Who are you? Write down everything about yourself that comes to mind. Do not censor yourself. If this seems like a daunting task, start by writing "I am, I am, I am" repeatedly until you think of something to write, even if it's "I am feeling silly right now" or "I am tired." Soon the words will flow.

Describe your perfect self. What do you like about yourself? Describe your imperfect self. What do you dislike? What talents do you have? What do you do well? What do you believe some of your shadows to be? What is your current attitude toward your shadow? Can you see any purpose in your shadow? What is it?

Why did you select this book? What do you hope to gain from your shadow work? What do you envision for your future as a result of shadow work? What do you hope for? Date the entry and save it.

The Star of Discovery

The Robin Wood deck is used in this book, but any deck that appeals to you is a fine substitute. Pull out the twenty-two major arcana cards numbered 0 to 21, the Fool through the World. Refer to Appendix A if you are unfamiliar with tarot. This workbook does not use traditional tarot card definitions. Instead, it looks at the darker, shadow side of tarot symbolism. It is an application of tarot to shadow work. Only the major arcana cards are used because they symbolize our spiritual journey and shadow work is a spiritual endeavor.

The shadow meanings given in Appendix A are suggestions to unlock your intuition and start a dialogue between your conscious and unconscious self. They are not meant to be all inclusive. Meditate upon a card, as described earlier in this chapter, and let your inner wisdom guide you.

Shuffle, cut the twenty-two cards, and choose your six cards facedown in any manner that pleases you (no ritual you perform is sacred unless it is sacred to you). If space permits, place the layout on your shadow altar. Keep the layout visible as you journal and meditate. You may want to photocopy the Star of Discovery spread (see Figure One on the following page) and place it in your journal. Always write down and date your impressions. Leave the layout on the altar for a few days. Be patient, go slowly. Continue to enter insights and observations about the

FIGURE ONE—STAR OF DISCOVERY

layout in your journal. New information may surface over the next few days or even weeks.

As you shuffle, concentrate on discovery of the shadow. Try to refrain from indulging preconceived notions about which cards will appear in your layouts. It is helpful to say, "Tell me what I need to discover about my shadow." Chanting a phrase while shuffling helps you concentrate on the task at hand. Even simple phrases, such as "Tarot, tarot, tell me true, what do I need to know from you?" can be powerful focus points and assist you in concentration.

When you feel you have shuffled enough, choose six cards and place them according to the Star of Discovery spread in Figure One. Be sure the first card you draw is in position one, the second in position two, and so on. Turn your cards face-up and note your initial "gut reaction" to the overall spread. Does it surprise you? Why or why not? Do you like it? Are you worried about what some of the cards may mean? Do not censor your thoughts. First impressions are lasting impressions.

Now that you have a general reaction to the Star of Discovery spread, go back to the first position:

Position One—Denial: Gaze at the card and answer the position one
question: What negatives or positives do people point out to me
that I have trouble accepting? This is where you will discover
denial. What does position one represent in your life? What
problems or conditions would you rather avoid? Refer to Appendix A for tips and suggestions about possible real-life situations.
What are you afraid of discovering? What might be your "blind
spot" that blocks growth?

It takes great courage to be exceptional. What talents and abilities are you hesitant to develop? What are you holding back?
What compliments make you uncomfortable? Remember, the
answers you need lie within the energy of that tarot card. Stay
with the card. Make an entry in your tarot journal. Be patient.
Insights will come as you progress.

Position Two—Anxiety: When do I get nervous, anxious, touchy, or
sensitive with others? Here you will discover your anxiety. What
loss do you fear? Fill in the blanks: Fear of _____ causes me to
feel anxious. I am most anxious when _____. Try to describe
specific situations as you journal. Refer to Appendix A for assistance with the meanings of the cards and possible real life events.

Position Three—Inferiority: When do I most lack confidence? Here
you will discover your area of inferiority. What does position
three represent in your life? What event or situation from the
past may have caused this shadow to grow? Did your parents play
a role in this feeling? Make a journal entry.

Position Four—Anger: What qualities in a person do I most dislike or
have the most difficulty dealing with? The answer is the key to
discovering your anger and/or rage. Anger is fear in disguise and
you may find yourself most uncomfortable with position four.

If you are a woman, you were probably taught that "nice" little
girls don't get mad. Instead, you may have stuffed your anger

allowing it to boil inside of you. Anger takes its shadows in the form of angry diseases: gastric ulcers, high blood pressure, overeating, anorexia, alcoholism, drug addiction . . . and violent behaviors, such as self-inflicted wounds, physical abuse, and bulimia.

You are not blaming others at this stage or trying to fix anything. You are detached from the pain and safe. Write down what comes to mind.

Position Five—Secrecy: Look at the card in position five and ask: What do I rarely talk about with others? What are my secrets and my family secrets? Remember to focus on the tarot card as you journal. The answer to the question lies in the energy of that card. What do you fear people will find out about you? What is your deepest, darkest secret? What do you think would happen if someone discovered your secret? Would your life change? What from your past are you trying to hide, if anything? What secret does your shadow reveal?

Position Six—Self-loathing: This may be the most devastating shadow of all. If we cannot love and honor ourselves we cannot realize our highest potential. Being your own worst enemy effectively sabotages personal growth and renders you a helpless victim in your life. The first step toward self-forgiveness is discovering where your self-hatred lies.

Look at the card in position six and ask: When am I most dissatisfied with myself? What do I need to discover? Your harsh inner critic is not your friend. Your inner critic wants you to fail. If you disobeyed your inner critic, what would happen? What do you fear?

Feelings of unworthiness arise from childhood. Did anything in childhood teach you to dislike parts of yourself? What? How many times a day/week/month do you call yourself negative names ("You idiot, I am so stupid, if I had a brain I'd be dangerous.")?

The answers lie within the energy of the card in position six. Stay with the card and record your responses as a detached observer. Be patient. The answers will come.

When you can write no more, set the journal aside. Leave the Star of Discovery layout on the shadow altar where you can see it on a regular basis. Return to the card in position one when you feel rested. Use it as a meditative focus (see chapter 2). Do not try to "force" information. Breathe deeply and relax. Allow your mind to be still and receptive. Attune to the whispering of your inner wisdom. Journal again about additional insights gained from meditating with the card in position one. Do not censor your writing even if the information is unclear at this time. Meditate one by one with the cards in positions two–six. Enter new perceptions in the journal, just as you did with the card in position one. Is meditation helpful to you? Why or why not?

You've worked very hard to get to this point. Go for a walk, take a bubble bath, observe a cat. Participate in an activity unrelated to shadow work. Play. It's time for a rest. Record and date thoughts over time as they emerge from your unconscious. Be a detached observer and write about your Other as the images surface. You are well on your way to discovering the shadow . . . it has been in hiding for a very long time.

Other Shadow Work Activities

The shadow resides in your unconscious and there are many ways to unlock it. Depending on your preferences, you can write a story about the shadow, compose a song, pen a poem, dance as your shadow would dance, or draw a picture of it.

What would your shadow look like? What would it say? See if images emerge for creative expression while you meditate. Create a supportive environment with candles, incense, or flowers. The images you experience may be imaginary, real, or something in between. Typically, they will be the opposite of your own self-image. Not only negative, they can represent those qualities you have been conditioned to ignore, such as competitiveness. They may be forbidden subjects or ideas you have been taught to believe must remain unexpressed.

In making these images conscious through drawing and story, you can visualize your disowned parts safely, on a piece of paper. Allow the images and words to surface without critical editing. Stay with the feeling and do not judge the quality of the work. Tell your inner critic to be still. You are aiming for emotional expression. No one is going to grade the aesthetic value.

If a frightening image or idea emerges, such as abusive situations or rape, try to keep drawing or writing. The point of pain offers a path through the darkness and can offer the greatest healing energy. Tell yourself the image or idea is in the past and cannot hurt you today. Remember, you are safe and can choose to leave at any time.

From your initial drawing, story, poem, or song, you can develop a series to your shadow. The images, colors, words or notes may change, taking many forms, reflecting the healing process. Confronting the shadow side in this manner will help develop your own inner strength.

What music might represent your shadow? Some classical music, especially by Russian composers, is dark and foreboding. Mussorgsky's *Night on Bald Mountain* establishes a particularly spooky mood. Both Wagner's "Ride of the Valkyries" is intense and other-worldly, while Mozart's *Requiem Mass* broods with a cosmic anguish.

In modern music, Eric Clapton's "Cocaine" has a subtly sinister side to it. Many Country and Western singers have released songs about loss and pain, while Blues may get you in touch with profound sadness. No one sings of heartache better than k. d. lang: try any of her torch-song albums.

The goal of shadow work is acceptance and integration of the shadow, not rejection of it. For this reason, you may want to listen to the lyrics of the Rolling Stones' "Sympathy for the Devil." Even Frank Sinatra's album *Sings for Only the Lonely* has the wailing quality of a lone wolf. Many groups specialize in angry lyrics and angry songs can help you discover fear in disguise.

Play shadow music and dance until you drop (consult your health provider of choice before any strenuous exercise). Which type of music did you choose? Why? What form does your dancing take? What are your body postures? What does this reveal about your shadow?

These suggestions serve as a launching point for your own musical selections and preferences. Regardless of the music you choose, allow the tone and texture of it to envelop you. You are not selecting music as background noise for your daily life. Music as shadow work is a way of communicating with your unconscious and requires attention. Allow yourself to feel feelings you have been afraid to feel. Cry. Rant. Rave. Throw pillows. Wail. Be angry. Be sad. There is no way over, under or around the shadow. The only path to freedom is through the darkness.

Watch a Sunrise and Sunset

Go out in nature away from bright lights just before twilight when the shadows are longest.* Watch as twilight yields to darkness. Feel the darkness setting in around you. Are you afraid? What are you afraid of? Does the night comfort you? Why or why not? Stay awhile and contemplate the darkness. When you return home, make a journal entry about the experience.

Do the same at dawn and watch a sunrise. Notice how the darkness yields itself to light. What does this tell you about your shadow work? Can you appreciate holding the opposites of dusk and dawn? What other opposites do you naturally accept? What opposites do you resist? Day yields to night. Night gives way to day. Does this give you more insight into what your shadow might be? How? Write in your journal.

You are now ready to begin the process of recovering lost parts of yourself. You've worked hard to be here. Celebrate your courage.

---

* Be sure to choose an area you know to be safe and take a flashlight with you. If the place is remote or secluded, tell someone where you are going. Bring a cell phone. While this is a sad commentary on our times, your personal safety is a priority when choosing a location for the sunrise-sunset exercise.

Chapter 4

IN THE SHADOW OF THE STAR

If a way to the better be,
it lies in taking a full look at the worst.
Thomas Hardy

IN CHAPTER 3 YOU BECAME AN INTIMATE OBSERVER OF THE SHADOW. You are now ready to become better acquainted with the Other. The goal of chapter 4 is to examine the focused shadow. The questions to ask yourself throughout this phase of shadow work are: What are the unresolved inner conflicts? What are the unexpressed emotions? How does my past affect my present? You are not looking for ways to change at this point. You are recovering lost parts of yourself. Where have you been hurt? What needs attention? What has been neglected?

The Star of Recovery tarot layout, combined with guided journal and meditation exercises, will help you answer these tough questions. A related shadow play activity concludes the chapter.

Recovery

The Latin root of recovery is *recipere*, meaning "to receive or to take." To receive something is passive—you allow it to happen. To take is a deliberate choice requiring action. Recovery is learning to hold opposites; through the power of personal choice, you allow the flow and process of healing to begin, at once active and passive.

Imagine a woman drowning in a pool. No attempt at rescue can help her because she is flailing her arms, afraid and fighting. She then makes a conscious choice to relax. The moment she decides to let go and stop fighting, she floats to the surface and is pulled from the water.

Recovery from past hurts cannot be forced. By actively exercising our power of choice, we allow recovery to occur. To be in recovery is to accept the mystery of paradox.

The Star as Symbol

Chapter 1 introduced the star as symbol, a light that guides navigators in the night. The star is also a symbol of the spirit that shines despite the surrounding forces of darkness. Stars are part of the natural order of life. Your gift from the star is more than self-discovery; it is an awareness of yourself as part of the pattern of the whole sky. Chapter 4 allows you to find your own shining center: to recover the lost parts of you that lie hidden in the shadows.

Preparation

As with all phases of shadow work, begin by grounding, centering, casting the circle of protection, and repeating your affirmation: By embracing my dark shadows, I am healing and becoming whole. I am gaining wisdom and learning compassion. (Refer to chapter 2 for details.) At the very least, become aware of your breathing. Slow it down. Breathe deeply until you feel yourself relax.

Be in front of, or near, your shadow altar. If candles, incense, soft music, or flowers please you, use them. The goal is to alert the unconscious that you are entering sacred space. Be nonjudgmental and receptive.

FIGURE TWO—STAR OF RECOVERY

Allow the information to be absorbed, but tell your inner critic to be quiet. If you find your mind wandering, gently bring your attention back to slow, deep breathing (see "Dealing with Distractions" in chapter 2).

Place your layout on the shadow altar, just as you did in chapter three. Keep the spread visible as you journal and meditate. Photocopy the Star of Recovery for the journal, if you wish (Figure Two). Write down your impressions and date the entry.

Leave the layout on the altar for a few days. Continue to enter insights as they occur to you over time. Be patient—the answers will come.

Star of Recovery: The Focused Shadow

Position One—The Focus: Choose a specific card from the Star of Discovery spread in chapter 3. Select one that is worrisome, least understood, frightens you, or one particularly to your liking. (We hide our exceptional qualities, too.) Write down why you chose the card. This card represents the shadow self that most needs exploration now. Place it in Position One (see Figure Two). It is used for questions two through six: the focus.

Shuffle the remaining twenty-one cards, including the other five from your Star of Discovery spread. While shuffling, concentrate on the lost parts of yourself that you need to recover. Ask: What is the unresolved inner conflict? What is the unexpressed emotion?

When you feel you have shuffled enough, lay five cards out facedown in positions two through six as shown in the illustration. Be sure the first card you draw is in Position Two, the second in Position Three, etc. Turn your cards faceup and note your initial "gut reaction" to the overall spread. Does it surprise or frighten you? Are you pleased or relieved? Why? Do any cards repeat themselves? Don't censor your thoughts as you make a journal entry about your first impressions.

Position Two—The Past: Now you have a general reaction to the Star of Discovery spread. Return to Position Two. Gaze at the card and answer the Position Two questions: How has my past shaped (Card 1)? Denial, anxiety, inferiority, anger, secrecy, self-loathing; what lost parts of your past do you need to recover? What does card two represent in your past? How has it affected Card 1? For example, if you chose a card representing anger in Position One, how has the past contributed to the anger you feel? Refer to Appendix A for tips and suggestions on possible interpretations, but remember your initial impression about a card's significance is (almost) always correct. The still, small voice of wisdom speaks to you in whispers. If there's shouting, it's coming from your inner critic. The answers you need lie within the energy of that specific tarot card in Position Two. Stay with the card. Make an entry in your tarot journal. Be patient. Shadow work is slow. Learn to trust your shining center. The answers will come.

Position Three—The Present: What causes my (Card 1) in the here and now? What situation does this represent (real life issues, self-destructive behaviors, interpersonal conflicts, unexpressed emotions)? Chapter 1, "The Shadow in Daily Life," and Appendix A offer clues, but they serve as only launching points. Allow your unconscious to speak to you in whispers. Make an entry in your journal.

Position Four—The Need for Clarity and Insight: What do I need to recover from my (Card 1)? What is the key to understanding your focus card? What is required for insight to occur? To illustrate, if the focus card (Position One) represents anger, what will help you understand the true origin or source of your anger? What caused the anger? What parts of yourself you did you lose as a result of expending energy on your anger? The answers you need are in the Position Four card. Record your reactions.

Position Five—The Pain: How has my (Card 1) caused me pain? In what ways has this shadow's unconscious expression hurt me? For instance, if anger is in Position One, (the focus card), how has the anger hurt you? The unconscious expression of anger can take the form of angry diseases such as peptic ulcer, high blood pressure, arthritis, or alcoholism. When the shadow of anger is unknown and operating on an unconscious level, you may literally be "eaten alive" by its expression. Likewise, if the focus card is fear, how has the fear held you back from experiencing the fullness of life? In what ways has fear kept you frozen, unable to move? How has fear caused you pain? Note your thoughts, feelings, and reactions in the journal.

Position Six—The Gift of Wisdom: What is (Card 1) trying to teach me about myself? What is the lesson to be learned? What will I recover as a result of (Card 1's) lesson? What is the gift that lies hidden in the shadows? Let's say a card representing aggression is in Position One as the focus. What wisdom will be revealed by making the aggression conscious? (Leadership qualities or the ability to stand up for the oppressed are examples of gifts that can come to light from the shadow of aggression.) The answers you need are in the energy of the card in Position Six. Stay with the card. You are not trying to change anything at this point. The goal is to become better acquainted with the unconscious (or lost) parts of you. You are being a detached observer of your life. Make an entry in your journal.

Leave the Star of Recovery layout on the shadow altar where you can see it on a regular basis. After a period of rest, use the card in Position One as a meditative focus (see "Meditation and Tarot" and "Entering and Leaving a Card" in chapter 3). Do not try to "force" information. Breathe deeply and relax. Allow your mind to be still and receptive. When you find your mind wandering, gently bring it back to your deep breathing. Attune to the whisperings of your inner wisdom. Make additional entries in the journal. Do not censor your writing. What insights did you gain from meditating? If you do not find meditation helpful, why might this be so?

As time passes, select another card from the original Star of Discovery spread in chapter 3. Place it on Position One of the Star of Recovery layout. It becomes the new focused shadow. For example, if you first chose the card representing secrecy as your focus, select the one symbolizing denial the second time around. The selection order is your decision. You will be drawn to the lost parts that most need attention.

Using the other cards, shuffle and repeat the Star of Recovery spread. Do this until you have selected all six Star of Discovery cards from chapter 3 as the single focus. This will yield a lot of information about the Other. What have you recovered?

Take care of you. Play. Laugh. Caress a cat. Walk in nature. Participate in an activity unrelated to shadow work. Celebrate your courage. It's almost time to come into the light.

Shadow Play

Play is the exultation of the possible.
Martin Buber

The shadow resides in the unconscious, and tarot is only one way to unlock it. As we write, sing, listen to music, dance, and draw, we dig ourselves out of our denial, anger, fear, shame, secrecy, and self-loathing. Now it's time to play. Play? Yes, play.

Your harsh inner critic may balk at the notion of play. You might say to yourself, "Okay, I was following her up to this point, but now she's lost her mind. I'm an adult with responsibilities. Life is serious. I can't waste my time with play." You want to do something to improve your life, but you want it to be the *right* something. You yearn and strive and wish and hope. How can play be related to this serious business of shadow work?

Play unleashes creativity. As we serve our creative selves through play, we are freed from our ego's demands and allowed to merge with a greater source. This conscious merging of intuition and intellect gives us the perspectives needed to solve our life's vexing problems. In the paradox of shadow work, we must get serious about play. We are not losing our minds when we play—we are gaining our souls.

Everything we need to know about life we learned as a child. By the age of five, the socialized person has formed—and so has the shadow. We cannot grow into the person we think we are without developing a sense of who we are not. One is owned, me; the other is disowned, not me. When we are young, we are strengthened by resisting undesirable behavior. Later in life, this resistance becomes a cut-off quality. "I" steps forward to introduce itself. "Not-I" is shoved back into the shadow. "Not-I" is the lost part of you.

Shadow work is a conscious and intentional process that requires us to take up what we have previously rejected. We establish a new personal order that accounts for our destructive side. The goal of shadow work is to bring the darkness to light, the unconscious is made conscious. Play provides the forum within which pent-up emotions and feelings can freely express themselves. It brings repressed ideas, feelings, wishes, and memories of the past (the shadow) into consciousness. Shadow play is a cathartic act that releases healing energy. Best of all, shadow play can be fun.

A gentle reminder: You are not trying to change anything with shadow play, you are discovering and recovering the lost parts of you. Keep the work safe by grounding, centering, and casting the circle of protection. Repeat the affirmation: "By embracing my dark shadows I am healing and becoming whole. I am learning wisdom and gaining compassion."

It is essential to recognize the fear and opposition you may encounter. These energies have protected you since childhood and a part of you will perceive shadow play as dangerous. You may feel like a vulnerable child, expecting abandonment or catastrophe. You may negate your shadow with the harsh inner voice of the rational parent. A religious voice from childhood may admonish you: "Don't play with the devil."

During shadow work, if you experience depression, fatigue, a loss of energy, or seemingly irrational behavior, STOP. Reassess your readiness to meet the Other. It may be necessary to work first with the primary self who fears the shadow (see chapter 2, "How Sad Is Sad?"). The shadow is powerful and it takes self-awareness to process life-altering information. In the true paradox of shadow work (or play), the key to exploring the shadow is not to explore it; allow the process to unfold in its own time. Never force shadow work. If you question your readiness, wait before proceeding. Remember, you are trying to heal old wounds, not create new ones.

Come Out and Play

Shadows begin to grow in childhood. The purpose of this exercise is to help you focus on, and find value in your shadow. Think of it as exploring the forest of your psyche. In finding a way to make the shadow a peaceful companion, you learn how to make contact with the unconscious and survive. The shadow will be neither crushed under foot nor allowed to dominate. When we accept our untamed nature, the shadow, it liberates us. Fanaticism, destruction, and rage become self-mastery, leadership, and compassion. Are you ready to come out and play with the shadow?

Let's Make Believe

In chapters 3 and 4 you discovered your shadow and started to recover the lost parts of you. Set aside the cards from the Star of Discovery and Recovery spreads for use in this exercise. Imagine a beautiful toy chest, a place where you hide all your treasures. What does your toy chest look like? Describe it in detail. This represents you as you present yourself to the world: the perfect you.

Locate a box big enough to hold the eleven cards. It doesn't have to be fancy. An old shoebox will do. Decorate the outside to symbolize the self you show the world. You can paste magazine pictures, draw, cover it with velvet, it doesn't matter, as long as it shows the ideal you. Do you cook? Paste pictures of food. Are you a mother? Show children. Do you go to school? Draw books. These ideas will help you get started. Allow your creative self to emerge as you decorate your toy chest, the perfect you.

Place the cards from the tarot layouts in the decorated box. These are your toys, the self you hide from the world, the shadow. The cards symbolize the treasures found hidden in the dark. Stir the eleven cards inside the toy chest until they are thoroughly mixed. As you stir, say out loud, "I want my shadow back." Say it emphatically, much like a stubborn child intent on her toy ownership: "I want my shadow back."

Draw one card from your toy chest and look at it. This is the hidden treasure you want back now: the lost part of you that wants to come home. What card is it? What lost part of yourself do you want back now? Here are some examples: If the card you drew symbolizes denial, you want back the truth. If the card represents self-loathing, you want back self-esteem. If it shows mistrust, you want to reclaim a sense of safety. How does the shadow card differ from the toy chest, the perfect you? In what ways are the self you show the world and the face you hide from the world different? How does your outside differ from your inside? Realize you are looking at a disowned part of you; If you want back your power, you must first claim the shadow that blocks it. What is the gift that hides in the dark?

Next, you are going to create a conversation between you and the lost part of you. Did you have an imaginary friend in childhood? The one who listened to all your plans and fears? Enter into that state of belief again. This time, your imaginary companion is a puppet. It can be as simple or elaborate as you wish to make it. Remember, creativity unleashes healing energy and intuition. The puppet can be made from a white sweat sock or purchased from a toy store. The more involved you are with its creation, the more effective the dialogue.

Draw or sew a face on your puppet. This represents the card you drew from your toy chest and your shadow—the lost part of you. What does your puppet look like? Is it someone you know or a stranger? What color is it? Is it an animal? If so, what type? Does it have a name? If not, name it now. Is this puppet offensive to you? Does it make you sad or angry? Can you laugh at shadow puppet? Place it on your hand and hold it up to you. Have it move and come to life. Allow it to yawn and stretch.

Start your conversation by saying, "I want my shadow back." What do you say to your shadow as you look directly into its eyes? You can initiate a dialogue with the lost part of you by saying something like this to your puppet: "Remember the time Mom said I was a bad little girl because of _____? Well, I wasn't being bad. You caused all the trouble by _____." How does your shadow puppet respond to you? What is the sound of her voice? What does shadow puppet say? Is it critical? Selfish? Cruel? Timid? Arrogant? Coy? Angry? Sad? Afraid? Sarcastic? Take a moment to fully experience shadow puppet. Let your feelings come to the surface.

Ask shadow puppet what it needs from you. For example, if it represents aggression, start talking to it in your most ladylike, passive voice. Tell your shadow puppet why aggression is not acceptable to you. Explain this in detail. Then ask shadow puppet to respond. You may be surprised when the voice of power answers. The following dialogue offers clues to the lost parts of you:

Your perfect self: Look, pushy one, I'm really embarrassed when you erupt out of nowhere and get me in trouble at work. I'm not like that. What do you want from me?

Shadow puppet: I'm angry because I'm left out. I resent being ignored. The more I try to get your attention, the more you pretend I don't exist. You're always trying to change me.

How would you like it if every time you attempted to express yourself, someone tried to mold you into something else? It's insulting.

Your perfect self: What do you want from me? How can we exist together?

Shadow puppet: Well, I don't like the way you allow everyone to push me around at work. I'm being taken advantage of and it's getting worse. I suggest you listen to me once in awhile. Take me seriously because I'm trying to help you survive. Honor what I have to say. Acknowledge my existence and I won't have to attack you by surprise anymore.

Your perfect self: Okay, okay. I'm tired of being everyone's doormat. If I allow you into my life, you'll stop erupting out of nowhere—and I might find my voice of power, after all.

Your dialogues will be different, of course, but if you ask the shadow what it needs, you may find treasures hidden in the dark. You can create shadow puppet dialogues with any (and all) of the cards from the first two tarot layouts.

Make an entry in your journal. Allow the words to surface without critical editing of your inner vision. Try to stay with the feelings of the dialogue. Did it surprise you? Why? How was your toy box (your conscious self) different from your shadow puppet (your unconscious self)? Did you feel silly playing with a puppet? Did it embarrass you? Why or why not? If you decided to skip shadow play because it felt ridiculous, clearly state in your journal why it was _____ (e.g., "stupid," "a waste of time," etc.). What is the resistance? Is your child lost? What could the shadow be telling you about creativity, spontaneity, and imagination? Did the decorations on your toy box (the perfect self) seem out of place after the dialogue, or no longer fitting? Why or why not? How would you decorate the box differently after shadow play? What does this reveal about the lost parts of you?

You have discovered and recovered the shadow. Part II, chapters 5 through 8, starts the process of acceptance, healing, integration, and change. Celebrate your courage in the dark . . . and step into the light.

PART II

INTO THE LIGHT

Chapter 5

YOUR SHADOW'S POWER

When an inner situation is not made conscious,
it appears outside as fate.
C. G. Jung

THE GOAL OF CHAPTER 5 IS TO ESTABLISH COMMUNICATION BETWEEN the intellect (conscious mind) and the nonrational mind (the unconscious). Defensive barriers soften so the shadow can emerge into the light and be understood. Common coping strategies are examined: what happens when we refuse to meet the shadow? Activities in chapter 5 include a tarot dialogue meditation called "The Shadow Speaks." This conversation strengthens the connection between your intellect and unconscious and coaxes the shadow out from its hiding place.

The personal shadow resides in the unconscious and is accessed by dreams, art, fantasy, daydreams, fairy tales, and myth. Dream work is explored because dreams are doorways to this mysterious shadow world. Suggestions for keeping a dream journal, incubating a tarot dream, and painting sacred dream art conclude chapter 5 as you come to understand your shadow's power.

The Intellect at Work

If the personal shadow resides in the unconscious, then the conscious self, or ego as Jung would say, serves as its gatekeeper. Most of the time, the rational mind is resistant to communicate with the nonrational mind. We develop coping strategies or defense styles which help us survive painful—even horrific—situations. Defense mechanisms protect us from fear and anxiety. For example, when we bury uncomfortable feelings such as sadness, anger, grief, or despair, the powerful shadow may emerge as depression.

The shadow never lies about itself, it is the ego (or acceptable parts of the conscious mind) that lies about its real motives. The shadow is not negative. The intellect, in its refusal of insight, contributes much more to unhappiness than the shadow. Jung wrote that the shadow is 90 percent pure gold.[1] Whatever has been repressed holds a tremendous amount of energy with great potential for growth. The path to healing—and freedom—is through the darkness. The only requirement for chapter 5 shadow work is a willingness to be honest.

Common Coping Strategies

In an attempt to feel safe, protected, and loved, we learn at a young age how to present ourselves to the world. We conceal our unacceptable parts in the shadow. We show the acceptable behavior to parents and teachers. It is here the shadow is born.

Coping strategies, or defense mechanisms, are any enduring patterns of protective behavior designed to defend against anxiety-producing awareness. Defense mechanisms are unconsciously motivated and acquired.* Coping strategies develop for the sole purpose of protecting the self (or ego) from unpleasantness and pain.[2] In the paradox of shadow work, we defend against the shadowy parts, and in this defense, the shadow is born and grows strong. Common defense mechanisms are listed below.[3] A tarot card exercise follows each description.

---

* We can thank the Viennese neurologist Sigmund Freud (1856–1939) for the first descriptions of defense mechanisms. While he identified eleven defense mechanisms, the seven most common are explored here. His major contributions to understanding the

Note: The tarot exercises are most effective when they are begun in a state of relaxation and centeredness. Start by placing the twenty-two cards of the major arcana before you.

Take some slow, deep breaths to achieve a state of relaxation. Light candles and burn incense to alert your unconscious that you wish to communicate with it. Repeat the shadow work affirmation: "By embracing my dark shadows I am healing and becoming whole. I am gaining wisdom and learning compassion."

Denial— Problem? What Problem?

When we disavow our thoughts, feelings, wishes, or needs that cause anxiety, we are in denial. For example, an alcoholic who is still drinking will defend against this troublesome knowledge by denying the problem exists. The person is not trying to be dishonest. It is an unconscious operation and functions to "deny" anything that cannot be dealt with on a conscious level—for whatever reason.

Shuffle the twenty-two tarot cards facedown. Concentrate on the information you need to know now about denial. When the time is right, pull one card out and look at it. What card did you draw? Is it the same card you drew for position one in the Star of Discovery spread in chapter 3? Cards that repeat themselves carry extra weight because they are trying to tell you about the recurrent themes of your life. They can also signify problems (or solutions) that require exploration for continued growth. A repetitive card can mean a block or "blind spot" to be resolved before answers are found. Whatever the reasons, repeating cards are important and are trying to convey information you need now.

Gaze at the card. If you find your mind wandering, bring it back to your slow, deep breathing. Answer the following questions in your journal: What does this card represent in my life? What problems or

human mind include: a penchant for exploring the deep layers of the psyche and the unconscious; psychoanalytic therapy as a means of changing thought, feeling, and behavior; an abiding concern with the symbolic, including dream interpretation; and a strong presumption that early childhood experiences influence us later as adults.

conditions would I rather avoid? What am I afraid of? What might be the "blind spot" that blocks my growth? Where is denial operating in my life? Remember to consider denial of talents and abilities; we hide our exceptional qualities, too. Don't censor your writing. Refer to Appendix A for meanings.

Repression—
Out of Sight, Out of Mind

Repression is an unconscious process that protects us from ideas and memories that would produce fear or anxiety should they become conscious.[4] In other words, painful stuff, and everything that reminds us of the pain, is pushed outside of awareness. When we say, "That didn't happen," (when in fact it did happen), we are repressing painful memories. It also means expelling from consciousness any natural desire that offends us, such as expressing anger or exhibiting sexual behavior. We repress natural desires to feel more acceptable and avoid the judgment or blame of others. This negative, unlovable shadow content is stuffed into the unconscious—out of sight, out of mind.

The problem arises because repressed memories and behaviors don't go away. They remain active in the unconscious. Since they are denied a controlled or regulated expression, they can explode at any moment in uncontrolled and even violent forms of behavior. The next time you find yourself shaking your head and saying, "What ever possessed me to _____?" the shadow of repression may be showing.

Understand that negative memories are repressed in order for us to function and survive. If you aren't ready to remember a painful experience, it is unwise to force it. Retrieving lost memories of rape, or sexual/physical abuse in childhood needs to be done in an atmosphere of trust and support. It may be unwise to try alone (reread "How Sad is Sad?" in chapter 2). Use your best judgment in deciding if it is time to uncover painful memories. You are trying to heal old wounds, not create new ones.

Shuffle the twenty-two tarot cards and select one without looking at it. Turn it over. What card did you receive? Record your instantaneous, "gut" reaction in the journal. If the card makes no sense to you, it may represent a deeply buried memory. Meditate with the card as a focal point. Be sure to ground, center, and cast your circle of protection when working with repression. Free associate in your journal—start by simply describing the card. What is the atmosphere and general feeling of the card? When have you felt this way? Start writing without censor. Write anything and everything that comes to mind. What feelings does this card produce in you? Do these feelings remind you of anything from your past? If it makes you fearful, write the word "fear" at the top of your journal page. Record every single thing that pops into your head as you look at the word fear. Read it aloud. Are you starting to see connections between the symbolism of the card and a real event in your life? Does it make sense to you now? Don't force memory—allow it to surface in its own time.

If this card represents an undesirable behavior (and not a bad memory), what might that behavior be? What are you stuffing? If you are passive, could you be stuffing aggression? If you are depressed, are you stuffing anger or rage? Say to yourself: "All this is me." What shadowy part of you needs to be owned, honored, and recognized, so you can step into the light and be free?

The end of this chapter offers suggestions for incubating dreams. You may want to program a dream about this card to obtain more information. If you do suddenly remember a horrific event from your past, seek support of some type to assist you in processing the event. Appendix B is a launching point for getting help. You do not (and should not) have to face the pain alone.

Regression—
Peter Pan is Alive and Well

Oh, to be a child again. Regression is the stuff of midlife crises. Adults sometimes behave like children in an attempt to get their own way or hide the frustration of aging and lost youth. Regression means retreating or going backward and is the opposite of progression. It's a stuck place and halts or slows growth.[5]

In the movie *Father of the Bride, Part II*, Steve Martin's character regressed to youth. When he discovered both his wife and daughter were pregnant, he dyed his gray hair and started behaving like a teenager. Regression is an unconscious attempt to maintain the status quo or return to a more pleasant time. Stop the clock and don't let anything change. Control, control, control.

When a spouse threatens to go home to mother or an adult stomps and screams to make a point, regression is operating. As children we may have succeeded in getting our way by temper tantrums and threats. As adults, this type of behavior suggests immaturity. Any kind of frustration in a situation can produce regression. Stress or anxiety can cause an adult to flee into a more immature state or earlier form of thinking.

Regression is the Peter Pan of defense mechanisms—an unwillingness to confront our life's problems and assume responsibility for our choices because of fear, anxiety, or stress. It is a stubborn refusal to meet the shadow and an attempt to control the hands of time.

Take slow deep breaths to reach a state of relaxation. Mix the twenty-two tarot cards facedown. Concentrate on the information about regression you need to know now. When you feel you have shuffled enough, randomly pull one card facedown from the deck. Turn it over. What card did you draw? Record your initial impression of the card in the journal. Does it surprise or bother you? The card you drew will either describe a situation where regression is operating or give you advice about that situation. What circumstance in your life does the card symbolize? Does it describe your plight or offer advice about it? Refer to Appendix A if need be, but trust your inner voice of wisdom.

Under what conditions does your temper flare? Have you thrown a tantrum lately to make a point? If not, has there been a time when you wanted to kick and scream? When? Describe it. What situation causes enough stress, anxiety or fear that you retreat to an earlier form of thinking? What is changing in your life? Do you wish to stop the clock? Why? What are you holding back? What do you need to control?

Do not edit your writing. Record everything that comes to mind. Stay with the card you drew. The needed answers are within the energy of that specific card. You are learning to trust the wisdom of tarot and your own intuition. What is this shadow trying to tell you? Does a particular area of your life need attention now? What is it? Repeat the affirmation: "By embracing my dark shadows I am healing and becoming whole. I am gaining wisdom and learning compassion." Honor all information you receive because the shadow is 90 percent pure gold.

Reaction Formation— Hurts So Good

Reaction formation is a defense mechanism with a vengeance. If a desire or drive produces anxiety, a person will overcompensate by developing its opposite. For instance, a man who feels himself to be physically inferior may become an intellectual or workaholic. A more common reaction formation is being afraid of sexual desire or preference. In this state of fear, a person can emerge as a stern campaigner against pornography, prostitution, sex outside of marriage, or sex education in the schools.[6] Reaction formation may compel a man with deep homosexual feelings to join an activist group against gay rights.

The problem, of course, is the intense feelings and desires don't go away. They are pushed into the unconscious and the shadow is born. The more we fight with the impulse and react against it with its opposite, the stronger it grows. As Shakespeare might have phrased it, when "the lady doth protest too much," we can reasonably suspect a reaction formation.

Take slow deep breaths to achieve a state of relaxation. Disconnect the phone. Light candles or incense to cue your unconscious that you wish to make contact with it. Repeat the shadow work affirmation. Shuffle the twenty-two cards of the major arcana and draw one facedown. Turn it over and record your initial overall impression of it in your journal. Gaze at the card and continue to breathe in a slow, deep way.

What card did you draw? As you look at the symbolism of the picture, what are your feelings? What situation does this card represent? Make a list of your causes, beliefs, or philosophies. Is there a cause or group that brings out intense feelings? What could these intense feelings be hiding? What desire or past regret lurks in the shadow? For example, a woman with conflicted feelings about having an abortion may become a pro-life activist. The pro-life activities cover up the unresolved issues surrounding the abortion. The more she tries to bury the past, the more intense her work becomes with the pro-life group.

The real problem—feelings of conflict surrounding the situation—is not faced. Because the true issue causing the pain never surfaces, healing cannot occur and the shadow grows. The more intense the pain, the more furious the activity until it becomes a vicious cycle of pain—activity; more pain/more activity. Reaction formation is a type of "running away" from the feeling, desire or pain. Think of your life as you look at the card. Are you fleeing from anyone or anything? Who or what? Write your thoughts, feelings, and reactions in your journal.

Identification—
Will the Real Me Please Stand Up?

The word has become a part of our everyday vocabulary. Identifying with a hero—pop star, film star, professional athlete, etc.—is a well-known phenomenon. But as it relates to shadow work, identification is not just hero-worship. It includes seeing oneself as the admired person, adopting his style of dress or hair, holding the same attitudes and beliefs. Imitating someone to get what we want is a form of identification. False flattery to achieve a hidden agenda is also a type of identification. In extreme cases, we will identify, or establish a link, with an aggressor to survive.[7]

The problem arises when we identify so strongly with a person or group, we end up not being our authentic selves. Intense identification keeps us from expressing our originality and fulfilling our own potential. At the end of a 1950s TV game show called "I've Got a Secret," the emcee asks that one of three impostors reveal himself as the true guest. And so it is with identification: Will the *real* self please stand up?

After centering yourself with slow, deep breaths, randomly select one card from the pile of twenty-two. Turn it over and record your immediate reaction to it. What card is it? Ask yourself: In what situations or relationships do I not speak my truths? Where do I hold back? Where do I feel a strong need to "fit in"? Do I identify with a person or group to the point of losing my authenticity? What are my beliefs? Do I compromise so much that I am no longer me? Do I use false flattery to get my own way? What would happen if I asked directly for what I needed? What shadow am I hiding? Will the real me please stand up? Make an entry in your journal and date it.

Projection—
You Are What I Think You Are

Projection is ascribing our own traits, emotions, dispositions, beliefs, needs, or desires to another. There is an accompanying denial that we ourselves have these tendencies or feelings. The projection protects us from anxiety and fear. Saying "He's arrogant" may really mean "I feel inferior." When a teenage girl complains that boys are always "hitting on" her (asking for sexual favors), she is projecting onto others a desire she refuses to acknowledge in herself. Taken to the extreme, projection allows us to blame others for all our problems.[8]

The causes of our difficulties are "out there" somewhere. When we project our woes onto the job, the relationship, the spouse, the bills, the kids, the illness (fill in the blank), we fail to look inside for the real solutions. Another way to project our fear onto another is by using hurtful, hateful words to describe the other. For instance, when we call a woman a "bimbo" (or any term we choose to use), we are projecting our own prejudices of womanhood onto her. She is not a bimbo—we have projected our negative feelings about femininity towards her. Racial or ethnic jokes and all stereotypes are forms of projection. Classifying a person or group of people with hurtful names says much more about us and our fears than it does the recipients of those labels.

As with all tarot exercises, begin by reaching a relaxed state of consciousness through slow, deep breathing. Shuffle the cards and randomly select one facedown. Turn it over. What card did you receive? Make an entry in your journal. Describe your initial response to it without looking up its meaning in Appendix A. How does it make you feel? Does it bring up negative ideas? Does it disgust you? What feelings about yourself could you be projecting onto another? What shadow of yours is being hurled across the room towards someone else? What would happen if you stopped looking outside yourself for solutions? Where would the answers be found?

Because denial accompanies projection, this defense mechanism is difficult to soften.* If you are stuck, make a list of people and behaviors

---

* No one will have every defense mechanism operating in his life. The purpose of these exercises is to help you identify the ones which may be active, so the barriers can soften—and as a result, the shadow is allowed into the light.

you don't like. Be specific, such as, "I can't stand it when people gossip." With your completed list of dislikes, study the tarot card you drew for projection again. Does it start to make more sense? When you look at someone you don't like, can you see any of yourself looking back? Record your thoughts and feelings in the journal.

The reward of coaxing projection out of its hiding place is great. When we begin to carry the shadow consciously, its burden no longer falls on others. We begin to give the impression of being more complete and therefore wiser. The beauty of shadow work starts to emerge; by carrying the burden of our own human weakness, other people are relieved of it. Personal wounds and relationships can begin to heal.

Somatization— Body Works, or Isn't Illness Handy?

When you go to the doctor because your neck hurts and the real problem is your boss is being a pain in the neck, you are suffering from somatization. It is characterized by chronic, recurrent, and multiple physical symptoms such as complaints of vague pain, allergies, gastrointestinal disorders, heart palpitations, or sexual dysfunction with no apparent organic cause.[9]

Like dreams, somatization is expressed in symbolic form. A gifted pianist suddenly unable to move his arm may express the musician's repressed desire to get away from the pressures of rehearsing and performing. A case of laryngitis before a presentation at work may hide the fear of public speaking. If our lives are insanely busy, a good case of the flu gives us permission to slow down and pamper ourselves. In other words, physical symptoms can be a conscious expression of an unconscious wish or desire. Illness can also prevent emotional pain from coming to the surface.

The problem arises because whatever is causing the psychic discomfort is not looked at directly. The vicious cycle of fear/emotional pain/unexpressed desire/illness remains unbroken. Our true needs do not get met. And so the shadow grows—until illness and its expression is the only way we know how to take care of ourselves or ask for what we need.

Concentrate your attention on breathing. Slowly breathe in and out until you feel yourself relax. Select one card facedown from the twenty-two major arcana cards to represent the coping strategy of somatization. What card did you draw? Make a first impression entry in your journal. Stay with the energy of that card. Take a slow deep breath and ask yourself: Where is my pain? Do I get sick a lot? Can I trace the timing of my illness to a specific uncomfortable event? What might my body be trying to tell me about unexpressed emotions and unresolved conflicts? How are my needs being met through illness? Does illness have a reward for me? What is the reward?

If you wish to explore this further, make a list of your physical complaints. Do any of them have a literal translation? For example, if you have heart problems, could it really be an expression of a broken heart? If you suffer from ulcers, is something eating you alive? Does high blood pressure mean someone makes your blood boil? Do respiratory problems symbolize your true feelings of suffocation or being trapped? Do your headaches represent the fact your job is a royal pain? As we shall see with dreams later in the chapter, the best place to start decoding your illnesses is with the literal translations. What is your body trying to tell you?* Stay with the selected card. The answers you need are in the energy of that card. Make an entry in your journal.

The Danger of Rationalization or Excuses, Excuses

Rationalization literally means consciously making up excuses for ourselves. A recent TV commercial shows a father questioning his daughter about a less-than-stellar report card. The teen responds with, "Well, it's your gene pool, isn't it?" That's rationalization and it serves to conceal our true motivations.[10] We know we are hiding our true feelings when we make up excuses. We make a conscious choice to evade the truth. It's convenient and it costs us our authenticity in the long run.

I prefer to call rationalization the "if only" syndrome. If only my job were better, I'd quit drinking. If only my relationships would smoothe

---

* If you are having ongoing physical symptoms, seek the advice of a health professional before assuming somatization.

out, I'd start that exercise class. If only there were less stress in my life right now, I'd stop smoking. Excuses stop us from being all we can be. Our lives pass before us as we wait for the Right Moment to change.

The truth is there will never be a Right Moment to change. Life will keep getting in the way.

If you believe the Right Moment to change is now, make an entry in your journal. At the top of the page place a heading called "Excuses, Excuses." On one side write this sentence: I can't _____ because of _____. List every single thing you can't do and why you can't do it.

On the other side of the page, write: I have to _____ because _____. Fill in those blanks, too. Record every demand that is placed upon you and why you must do it. Don't censor your writing. Take some time with this. Run through a typical day and think about all the times you say "yes" and "no." Make no judgments. This is only an information-gathering exercise. Save your list. You will use it in the next section called "Bright Shadow."

Bright Shadow

Superman must hide his good qualities under the guise of Clark Kent. Unclaimed talents and abilities are called the bright shadow.[11] It does take courage to be exceptional; others may project their own dark shadows of envy or perfectionism on us when we succeed. Any creative talent we have not developed, or one that has gone unexpressed for whatever reason, is the bright shadow: more lost parts of ourselves.

Our potential talents seek to live and need an outlet. Our unexpressed creativity will tolerate repression for just so long. Eventually these stuffed energies (creative impulses) will appear as irritability, depression, or fatigue—until they are given attention and some form of expression.

When we project the bright shadow onto someone else, the person who carries the projection will seem able to do things better than we can and always be right. We burden him with our expectations of perfection. When we cast a bright shadow on another, we do not acquire for ourselves the possibility of developing the potential within us.

When we project our bright shadows onto our neighbor, we become content to take an inferior position or to have an easy job rather than developing our full potential. We will overadmire someone else who does these things well. And we pay the price, ending up depressed, irritable, and fatigued. Make a conscious decision to reclaim the lost parts of you—today—so healing can begin.

Pull out the list from the previous section: all the reasons you can't do some things and must do others. At the top of the next page, write: My Wildest Fantasy. What have you always wanted to do? What is your dream job? If you could do anything or be anything, what would it be? Don't hold back—this is supposed to be fantastic. If you find your harsh inner critic screaming at you (with words such as "ridiculous" or "stupid"), tell it to be seated. This is not an exercise for your harsh inner critic. All your unexpressed talents want to come out and play.

If you have trouble starting, begin with "I am good at _____." Or, "I have always enjoyed _____, but I don't do it any more." Another tack is, "People have always told me I have talent and should be a _____."Try "When I was a kid I wanted to _____ when I grew up because _____." Let your imagination run wild. If you always wanted to be a painter, musician, writer, or gentleman farmer, write it down. This is your fantasy and not subject to ridicule. Don't hold back.

Now shuffle the twenty-two tarot cards and select one randomly, facedown. Place it on top of your excuses list from the last section. It represents the shadow of rationalization; the reasons you can't do some things and must do others.

Next, choose another card facedown and place it on top of your wildest fantasy list. It symbolizes the shadow that prevents you from expressing your talents and creativity—your bright shadow. Reread both lists to refresh your memory.

Turn the cards over and compare. Is there a stark difference or are the two cards similar in meaning? Can you see a connection between the excuses you make for yourself and the bright shadow? Do the reasons you can't do some things look like the reasons you haven't developed your talents and abilities? What part does fear play in both lists? What is holding you back? By comparing your list of excuses and the list of fantasies, can you start to see a relationship between the two? If one of your excuses is that you have no time to pursue creativity, where should you be saying "no" more often? Make an entry in your journal.

If the tarot card meanings are unclear to you, try meditating with a specific card as the focus. (See "Entering and Leaving a Card," chapter 3.) It may be time to encounter the Dark Goddess again, as you did in chapter 2. What new gifts of understanding does she give you from the shadows? Ask for her help and wisdom. Meditate before your shadow altar. Don't try to force information—become willing to submerge into the darkness to meet the Other. Go to a bookstore and browse the tarot section. See where it leads you. Trust that the information you need will become available to you in the most understandable form possible at the right time. (Isn't trust the hardest part?) *Tarot Shadow Work* is an application of tarot and not a tarot "text" of basic definitions. Look in the back of this book. Appendix C offers suggestions for branching out and reading more.

The task of shadow work is ongoing. The shadow contains not only our dark side, but energy, vitality, and imagination. As each layer is explored, each projection reclaimed, and each fear is faced, the gifts of the shadow emerge. The shadow has no bottom, yet, somehow, as we embrace the darkness with compassion, the light starts to shine through.

In the next section, the shadow speaks and you will learn to communicate directly with it without fear.

Conversing with the Shadow

The use of active imagination in this exercise will coax the shadow out of its hiding place. The purpose of active imagination is to interact with the unconscious.[12] The aim is to begin the integration of the shadow. One way to work with the shadow (or unconscious) is to create a conversation with the Other.

Dialogues with shadow characters can reveal a wisdom you didn't know you had if you can loosen up to hear the messages. You may be concerned you are "making this up" as you go along. You are—but it's coming from your higher source of wisdom. If you can suspend disbelief and listen to what the voice of Other says, you will hear what you need to hear and gain a new perspective on your life.

You may be fearful to meet the shadow. What might you find out about yourself? What memories or feelings will come up? Tell yourself anything that happens is only temporary. As with all shadow work, even a scary experience is trying to inform you of something important about your life. It is helpful to think of shadow dialogue as a gift: you will uncover significant insights that you can use to heal and move towards freedom.

Getting in touch with the shadow of anger, fear, aggression, etc., and making it conscious is the best way to keep these emotions and urges in check. The "Shadow Speaks" exercise is designed to give these feelings a safe place for expression. Pushing them out of awareness makes them stronger. When you mindfully explore the shadow and allow it a voice, you will also have an opportunity to see parts of yourself that you treasure: the "Bright Shadow" and the lost parts of you. It may be helpful to repeat: "All this is me."

A receptive mood is essential for active imagination. People who are threatened when they aren't in total control may find the "Shadow Speaks" dialogue difficult. Go slowly. Be open to the chance of establishing a relationship with the lost parts of you. Suspend your need to disbelieve.

It is important to know what you are dealing with here; you have called up an energy that is either giving you some difficulty because it has been denied and repressed; or, you may overvalue it so it has become tyrannical. It can be powerful. You need to be receptive, yet firm and watchful as you converse with the lost parts of you. When you question your shadow, wait for a response. Responses will vary from person to person. You may hear an answer, feel an impression, or see something. You may envision a symbol or a location. It is common to not understand the message immediately. You may have to meditate with it or incubate a dream, as you will learn to do at the end of this chapter. Be patient. The answers will come.

Preparation for Speaking with the Shadow

It can be powerful or scary when you hit areas of inner pain. Touch base with a trusted friend or professional when doing this work. Always enter active imagination with a protective energy. Ground and center. When you cast the circle of protection, ask that the circle be neutralized of all incorrect energies; and, that the circle be filled with only the most perfect, powerful, correct, and harmonious energies compatible with your purposes of shadow work.[13] Repeat the shadow work affirmation. Add this: "I ask to be led to my highest level of awareness for my best possible good, its equivalent or better. Harm none. So must it be." There is much protection available in the inner worlds and the universe. Ask for it.

The Shadow Speaks

This exercise is different from the other tarot activities. You will not shuffle or have fate choose the cards for you. Instead, deliberately select two cards from the twenty-two. One represents the mask you show the world: the "I-card," the perfect you. The other symbolizes the face you hide from the world: the "Not-I" card, your shadow. You should relate to the first card in a positive way. The second (Not-I) picture makes you feel uncomfortable. It doesn't matter which cards you choose as long as you like the "I-card" and have some negative feelings about the "Not-I" selection. Be sure you have cast the circle of protection before proceeding. It may be helpful to tape-record the instructions that follow and play them back as you do the exercise.

Become aware of your breathing. Slow it down. When you have reached a state of calm relaxation, say out loud, "All this is me." Place the two cards before you so the border of each card is touching the other. In chapter 3 you learned how to enter and leave a tarot card. You will do this again, except you will be entering the two cards at the same time. The two cards with touching borders are now becoming one picture.

Gaze at the cards until the touching borders become fuzzy or indistinguishable. Imagine you now have one scene before you. Don't strain your eyes. Allow it to happen through your slow, deep breathing. Take the time necessary for this merging. When the picture is as one, allow the single scene to enlarge. You are about to enter sacred space and have a conversation with the Other.

In your mind's eye, step through the border of this one picture. Look around you and observe: What is the atmosphere in this place? Do you sense conflict or chaos? Are the characters afraid or cautious of one another? Is the mood or feeling one of apprehension? Cautious tolerance? How do the people or things in the scene interact—or do they? Is the air charged, stagnant, or calm? For example, if you chose an "airy" card such as Justice (11) and a "watery" card like the Moon (18), how do air and water mix? If you selected the Sun (19), a "fiery" card, how would it interact with an "earthy" card such as the Empress (3)?

It's time to initiate a dialogue between these two characters (cards): The "I-Card" represents your rational mind or intellect, the mask you show the world.* You will speak for this character. Assume the attitudes and stance of the characters in the "I-Card." Start a conversation with the Other (the "Not-I" card) by asking direct questions. Trust your intuition and wait for answers. You are speaking to the shadow now. Here are examples to get you started:

* Who are you?

* I have a question for you . . .

* What do you need to tell me?

* What have I been missing?

* How have I been ignoring you?

* Do you need something from me? If so, what?

* At what phase of my life were you born?

* How did you grow?

* What lost part of me do you represent?

Gaze directly at the card representing the shadow as you ask the questions. Remain in a receptive and expectant mood. Write down every single thing that pops into your head, even if it makes no sense right now. Do not censor your writing. Your unconscious may speak to you in words, feelings, impressions, sounds, or symbols. The important thing is

---

* Jung would call the rational or conscious mind the "ego."

to refrain from judgment. Just write. It is the shadow's nature to hide. Coax it into the light with respect. Honor all information you receive and say out loud: "All this is me."

The shadow is done answering questions. Now it speaks for itself. Assume the attitudes and stance of the shadow ("Not-I") card: the face you hide from the world. For instance, if it's angry, speak in an angry voice. Look directly at the perfect self ("I-card") and let the shadow have its turn. Begin with statements like the following:

* I have come to tell you . . .

* I am angry at you because . . .

* I become aggressive when . . .

* I want . . .

* I need . . .

* I have . . .

* I have not . . .

* I desire . . .

* I represent this lost part of you . . .

* I protect you from . . .

Record all thoughts, feelings, impressions, and symbolism in your journal without censor. When you receive no more information, return your attention to slow, deep breathing. Remind yourself, "All this is me." Step back through the borders of the cards. Allow the cards to become two-dimensional and normal in size again. Put the palms of your hands on the floor and breathe deeply. This will ground you. Sit quietly for a few moments until you feel a return to normal consciousness. Place the two cards (the mask you show the world and the face you hide from the world) on your shadow altar for a few days. Continue to write down insights as they occur to you.

What was most surprising to you about this exercise? What was its value in understanding your shadow's power? Did it help to hear the shadow speak? Why or why not? Were you afraid? Did the exercise feel silly? Explain. What bit of insight can you carry with you into chapter 6—accepting your true self?

Remember that in your work you are trying to develop a positive relationship to inner energies that are not in balance. Listen to these energies express their frustrations. Try to help them find the right expression. By being both receptive and firm, your "ego-I" will not tyrannize and the "Not-I" shadow won't dominate. This integration can reveal gifts that hide in the dark.

The best way to coax the shadow out of its hiding place is to stay as close to the unconscious as possible. Journal writing, active imagination, meditation, and work with tarot all accomplish this task. Dream work is explored in the next section. Share yourself openly and honestly. Each time we push away an uncomfortable feeling or hold in words we need to say, we help the shadow grow. If we face our fears, pain, and anxiety on a regular basis, we are less likely to experience an eruption of the Other.

A Note About Dreams

If Viennese neurologist Sigmund Freud unlocked the secret door to dreams, then Carl Jung coaxed it open. Since then, many others have walked through the portals. Dream work pioneers include Fritz Perls, Ann Faraday, Jeremy Taylor, and Gayle Delaney.[14] Dreams and dream work are extensive topics. Our focus here is incubating tarot dreams. If you want to learn more, please refer to Appendix C. Joan Mazza's *Dreaming Your Real Self* (1998) is an excellent place to start.

Jung called dreams "the royal road to the unconscious"[15] and it is here the shadow resides. Some of the tarot symbolism from previous layouts may still be unclear to you. If a card from chapters 3, 4, or 5 continues to perplex you, dreaming tarot may provide the answers.

The Dream Belongs to the Dreamer

The only person who can interpret your dream is you. Dream interpretation needs to "feel right" to the dreamer. It is ultimately up to you to decide the truest meaning of a dream. Don't fall into the trap of supposing that this or that theorist (including Jung) has the whole truth. Take—from anyone—whatever makes sense to you. If you feel an approach does not go far enough, move to another one.

A book will tell you what interpretation you might give your dreams. Your dreams will tell you what interpretation you should be giving them. If a fox appears in your dreams, remember that Mother Nature didn't put a goose or a zebra there. Decide what the symbolism of the fox is for you. Dream interpretation is a cautious balance between logic and intuition. Don't overanalyze—if you get it wrong the first time, your unconscious will try again. Learn to trust the process. If you approach dream work with honesty and care, your dreams will do the rest.

When you first begin working with your dreams, stay in today. A dream from the past still portrays the issues that are unresolved or important to you in the present. We dream about what is uppermost in our minds. After you examine the here and now, you can look beyond the first and obvious layer. Issues that burden us our entire lives—such as problems with authority figures, coming to terms with trauma, living responsibly, or searching for spiritual answers—will be evidenced in our dreams. At one level, the dream may communicate the day's concerns and that is where you need to start the search. If you look closer, your life task or mission statement may also be reflected.

Start with the literal meaning of a dream. No matter what the content of a dream, examine the story exactly as it appears. For instance, if you dream the brakes of your car go out, you might want to get the brakes checked. Then look for life issue symbolism: Do you feel your life is without brakes, spinning out of control or about to crash?

Don't make any big decision based solely on one dream. Each dream is a piece of the larger puzzle of our lives. There are days when we hate our jobs and want to run away to Bora Bora, but that doesn't indicate the feelings of the moment are the entire picture. We love/hate many things. The dream may offer us the flip side of our situation but it's not telling us to take dramatic action. Instead, it reminds us to stay balanced and honest with ourselves.

The key to the significance of a dream is in the feelings it produces: Does the dream make you afraid, embarrassed, disgusted, confused, angry, sad, depressed, hopeful, or happy? The overall emotional state is important to assist you in making the connection between the dream and your waking life.[16]

Many books are available about dream objects and their symbolism. A dream dictionary can get you started, but you are the only person who can interpret your dreams accurately. Try making a personal dream dictionary. For example, you may notice certain objects appear over and over in your dreams. Obviously, these objects carry important meanings for you, but what? Let's say you dream repeatedly of a cat. You look up "cat" in a dream dictionary and it tells you a cat symbolizes your mother, feminine wisdom, femininity, the unconscious, nature's wisdom, or the ultimate mystery of life and death.[17] If you are afraid of cats in real life, the image may represent things you are frightened of in yourself. The significance of the cat can be recorded in your own dream dictionary, regardless of what the published books tell you.

If a red flower appears to you in a dream, ask yourself: What does flower mean to me? What does red signify in my life? When you start asking and answering questions like these, you are on your way to compiling a personal dream dictionary that can be studied over time.

Perchance to Dream

Dreams may represent literal concerns, have a predictive quality about them, illuminate life issues, assist in problem solving, highlight psychological issues, or simply be the residue of a stressful day. You may see persons who are no longer living or dream of a past life.[18] Whatever the reasons for your dreams, you can improve your ability to remember them by following a few simple techniques:[19]

* Get enough sleep. Nothing kills dream recall faster than fatigue. Avoid caffeine products in the evening. REM (rapid eye movement) sleep is the stuff dreams are made of. The REM state cannot be achieved when the brain is over-stimulated. Drink a cup of chamomile, valerian, or rosemary tea for relaxation before retiring.

* Repeat a simple affirmation as you drift into sleep: "Tonight I will remember my dreams." Or, make up a rhyme and chant it as you fall to sleep: "I wish I may, I wish I might, recall the dreams I dream tonight."

* Keep paper and pencil or a tape recorder by the bedside. Write down or tape the details of your dream the moment you wake up. (More about this in the dream journal section to follow.)

* Don't suffer from analysis paralysis. Meditate. Free associate. Ask yourself questions, but don't overanalyze the results. Tell your harsh inner critic to be still.

* Engage in right-brained activities: draw, paint, go to an art museum; read fairy tales and mythology; read poetry; better yet, write poetry; work with tarot, play a musical instrument, listen to music, compose a song, sing, dance, buy moulding clay and sculpt; finger paint, color with crayons, get messy. The more engaged your inner self is during waking hours, the more the unconscious will communicate with you in your dreams.

Keeping a Dream Journal

Prepare to encounter your own deep nature; expect a dream and the ability to recall it. Keep an open notebook (or tape recorder) by your bed. Next morning, the moment you awaken, record the dream exactly as you remember it. Try avoiding the bathroom first or having a cup of coffee to wake up. If you do, the dream will be lost. Don't move more than necessary.

If you can summon only the tiniest part of the dream, pull it back by that corner; in other words, bring that bit of dream fully into your memory, then recall the action just before. By starting with what you do remember and working your way backward, you can elicit the entire dream.

You are most likely to recall the last portion of the dream first. The tendency is to remember and write down all the sections of a dream in reverse order. Keep this in mind when interpreting a dream: look for a solution first and work your way backward to the problem. Date your dream journal entries. Don't be concerned with grammar, sentence structure, spelling, or penmanship. (You want to be able to read it later, of course.)

Write your dreams in the present tense: "I am walking on a deserted highway," not, "I was walking." Give titles to the dreams using the most important action or object, such as "Deserted Highway." Make marginal notes describing what is going on in your life at the time of the dream. For example, along the deserted highway dream, you might put "moving from the city this week," or whatever is happening right now.

Read your journal every few weeks. You may notice patterns, such as having vivid dreams during ovulation or when the moon is full. Knowing this, you can prepare for dreams on these nights. Look at several dreams together to see if there is a common pattern. You can use a technique for studying dreams called the dream-series method.[20] Keep a dream diary until fifty or more dreams have been accumulated.* The full set can then be examined for patterns, personal symbolism, and recurring themes. Compile your own dictionary of dream symbols from this information.

Keeping a dream journal is at once difficult and easy, in the true paradox of shadow work. Recording every detail of a dream the minute you wake up is the last thing most of us want to do immediately upon waking. But if dreams are not written down at once, they fade away like mist under the morning sun.

Dreaming Tarot

We understand tarot from the same place we dream—the unconscious. By engaging in tarot and dream work, we can connect directly with the shadow and coax it out of its hiding place. The tarot operates primarily through the symbolic, nonrational aspects of consciousness, the same state through which dreams communicate. As we advance our level of shadow awareness, our insights into dreams and tarot will reflect this expansion. Obscure symbolism will no longer baffle us. Tarot can be used at least two ways in conjunction with dream work: to represent a dream or to incubate a dream.

---

* This is your dream work. Work with the number of dreams that feels sufficient to you.

Representing a dream with tarot—Our dreams are great advisors, but sometimes, the symbolism or advice eludes us. Choose a tarot card which closely matches the theme of the perplexing dream. For example, if you have an angry dream, select a card that conveys anger. (See Appendix A, or better yet, use your intuition.) Take this card to bed with you. Tell the figure on the card what is going on right now and why you don't understand the specific dream. Ask a question: "What do I need to know about this dream?" Place your "guide card" under the pillow. As you drift to sleep, picture the guide card taking you by the hand and entering your dreams with you. When you wake, make an entry in your dream journal. The answers you receive are often very clear.*

Incubating a tarot dream—It is possible to request a dream about a particular card. Let's say you drew the Moon (18) for one position in the Star of Discovery spread (chapter 3) and its significance is still unclear. You can program, or incubate, a dream about the Moon, requesting more information.

As you prepare for sleep, envision the card in your mind's eye with as much detail as possible. Look closely at the card and notice everything you can about it: its tone, texture, colors, mood, atmosphere, the characters, objects, animals. Close your eyes and try to recall the whole card. Look at the card again and notice what you missed. Do this until you can view the entire card with your eyes closed.

Next, what feelings does the card invoke? Anger? Sadness? Joy? Fear? Confusion? Hope? Try to "feel the feelings." Allow them to be a part of you without trying to change them. Does the card remind you of a person you know or a situation in your life? Who or what? Think about this person or situation as vividly as you can while looking at the card. Write out in detail why this card puzzles you. Using the Moon as an example, you might write, "Well, a dog and wolf howling at each other with some kind of crustacean in the foreground makes no sense to me."

Formulate a specific question and be concrete—the unconscious mind is as literal as it is metaphorical. For instance, ask: "Show me a new

---

* You can also select a tarot card representing your dream and meditate with the card as the focus to gain insight into the dream.

way to understand this card." Or, "What information do I need from this card?" Repeat your question throughout the day. Write the question in your dream journal before going to sleep. Add: "I ask that this dream reveal the information I need now, in the most understandable form possible."

When you wake up, record whatever you remember about the dream, even if it appears nonsensical or unrelated to the tarot card. If it's about another subject, write it down anyway. Review the dream in terms of your request. It will probably be in symbol or metaphor. Going back to the Moon example, you may dream about deciding between graduate school and a good-paying job, but the dream is telling you something new and helpful about its meaning, if that's what you asked for. (The Moon, by the way, often conveys a sense of confusion or indecision, especially in the emotional realm.) So the new information in this dream is telling you the source of your emotional dilemma is a choice between education and money. The Moon, in this example, has revealed a conflict between your truest desire (the wolf) and what you think you "should" do (represented by the domestic dog). Trust that you will always get an honest answer, but not always the one you want.

What if a tarot card makes an unsolicited guest appearance in your dream? It does happen. If it does, go to your deck and select that card. Meditate with it as your focus. Give it a place of honor on your shadow altar. Ask it questions, draw it, free-associate with it, carry it with you during the day; but, whatever you do, don't ignore it.

It was in your dream for a reason. Dreams and tarot are wonderful advisors. By combining the power of the two, you have tapped into a wellspring of universal wisdom. Approach this power with respect and sense of expectancy.

A note about nightmares and recurrent dreams: Nightmares and recurrent dreams may leave us uncomfortable, frightened, confused, or anxious. They are a vivid call to arms that asks us to urgently look at what is happening and take action to change it. If you suddenly start having nightmares and you haven't had them before, ask yourself what has changed in your life. New medication, sugar, chemical additives or alcohol can cause nightmares; so can a new sleeping partner, increased stress levels, relationship problems, and financial insecurity.[21] Never discontinue a new medication without consulting your doctor first, as a sudden stop of certain medicines can be life threatening. Even positive changes in your life can bring on nightmares as you are adapting to the change. Talk it over with a trusted friend or health professional. Get advice. The nightmare or recurrent dream is trying to get your attention.

The best way to avoid nightmares is to stay in conscious contact with your unconscious. This means doing inner work on a regular basis through dream work, tarot, journaling, therapy, creative projects, and meditation. You can follow the steps described earlier to represent the nightmare with a tarot card for more information.

If we face fears regularly and take action to conquer them, we will be less likely to experience nightmares. Remember—there are no "bad dreams." If our inner self is trying to speak to us and we're not listening, it may have to shout to wake us up. When we pay attention and get the message, the shouting will stop.

The Sacred Art of Painting Your Dreams

Dreams have a literary, poetic, and artistic quality. They provide us with an opportunity to tap into our own inner wells of talent and wisdom. We become aware that dreams are sacred because they come from a deep source of knowing. When we paint or draw dream persons and symbols, we should not trivialize them as mere wall decorations. Our inner images are an intimate part of ourselves—displaying them casually for all to see is akin to showing our private lives to anyone who happens by.

Dream art is sacred because it directly expresses the Higher Self and inner source of wisdom. None of us would want to keep the door to the consultation room open while we poured our hearts out to the therapist. Likewise we should treat all dream productions as sacred and confidential. If someone ridicules your dreams or dream art, he is rejecting the deepest part of you. Sharing dreams and dream art needs to be done in an atmosphere of trust and support.

Dreams into art—select a dream that was particularly vivid. It can be from the past or present. Review the dream journal for details. You don't have to understand the dream to transform it into art; in fact, changing a dream into a painting or sculpture may assist you with insight. Recall the theme, strongest emotions, images, smells, sensations, and action: anything at all concerning the dream that makes it stand out among the others.

Start small. Choose one or two elements from the above suggestions to get you going. For example, if a dream animal frightened you, draw the animal or a metaphor of it. Explore its color, shape, size, smell, or sound. Engage all your senses in this creative project. Go to an art supply or craft store and look at the possibilities: painting, drawing, sculpting, watercolors, finger paints, crayons, molding plastics, clay, felt, magic marker, sparkles, buttons, stencils . . . the list goes on. Pick a medium that speaks to you and let your intuition and creativity flow. Any of these avenues of expression can be used as clues to uncover more layers of the dream. (And let's not forget it can be fun.)

Critical evaluation of your project has no place in the sacred art of painting dreams. Abandon the notion your creation should be aesthetic because it will hinder deeper understanding. (If your frog has warts, by all means, include the warts.) Dream art does not have to be flattering— only honest. It allows you to move from the very personal, going deeper and deeper, until you arrive at the sacred well of wisdom within.

In this chapter, you learned how to coax the shadow out of its hiding place and make a connection to the source of inner knowing. The shadow has been met. Celebrate your courage.

Endnotes

1. Zweig, Connie and Steve Wolf. *Romancing the Shadow*. (New York, Ballantine Books, 1997), p. 55

2. MacKinnon, Roger A., M.D., and Robert Michels, M.D. *The Psychiatric Interview in Clinical Practice*. (Philadelphia, W.B. Saunders Company, 1971), p. 81

3. Reber, Arthur S. *Dictionary of Psychology*. (New York, Penguin Books, 1985), p. 287

4. Thomas, Clayton L., M.D., editor. *Taber's Cyclopedic Medical Dictionary*, 17th Ed. (Philadelphia, F.A. Davis Company, 1993), p. 1697

5. Kaplan, Harold I., M.D. and Benjamin J. Sadock, M.D. *Synopsis of Psychiatry,* 6th Ed. (Baltimore, Williams and Wilkins, 1991), p. 183

6. Hunt, Morton. *The Story of Psychology.* (New York, Anchor Books, Doubleday, 1994), p. 202

7. Kaplan and Sadock, op. cit., p. 183

8. Morton, op. cit., p. 203

9. MacKinnon, op. cit., p. 406

10. Thomas, op. cit., p. 1675

11. Harding, Ester M., M.D. *The I and Not I: A Study in the Development of the Consciousness.* (New Jersey, Princeton University Press, 1965), p. 98

12. Gwain, Rose. *Discovering Your Self Through Tarot.* (Vermont, Destiny Books, 1994), p. 17

13. Cabot, Laurie. *Celebrate the Earth.* (New York, Bantam Doubleday Dell Publishing Group, 1994), pp. 261–262

14. Mazza, Joan. *Dreaming Your Real Self: A Personal Approach to Dream Interpretation.* (New York, Berkley Publishing Group, 1998), p. 2

15. Joy, Brugh. *Joy's Way.* (New York, G.P. Putnam's Sons, 1979), p. 76

16. Ackroyd, Eric. *A Dictionary of Dream Symbols.* (New York, Sterling Publishing Company, 1993), p. 4

17. Ibid., p. 113

18. Pascal, Eugene. *Jung to Live By.* (New York, Warner Books, Inc., 1992), pp. 248–252

19. Reber, op. cit., p. 216

20. Mazza, op. cit., p. 122

Chapter 6

EMBRACING YOUR SHADOW

Truly it is in the darkness that one finds the light,
so when we are in sorrow,
then the light is nearest of all to us.
Johannes Eckhart

Discovering the Light Within

CHAPTER 6 SHOWS YOU HOW TO HANDLE THE TENDER, NEWLY EMERGING self with the greatest of care. As you practice the exercises in this book, you may begin feeling exposed and raw. Shadow work takes tremendous courage. The time has come to start putting the pieces back together in a meaningful and realistic way.

The healing power of pure intention is explored as you learn to make direct contact with your Spiritual Source for guidance. The archetype of the Wounded Healer is examined and a visualization exercise starts the self-healing process. The Star of Illumination tarot layout offers you an opportunity to contact your own healing potential. You are the star of your own life. This chapter concludes with suggestions for creating realistic goals for change. The focus throughout is accepting your true self.

You have not gone over, under, or around the shadow, but directly through the darkness. The shadow has been embraced. As you discover the light within, you gain wisdom—and a sense of responsible, personal power.

Shadow Work is Soul Work

The ultimate goal of shadow work is to move through different levels of awareness, or consciousness, to reconnect with our Higher Self (the soul). Everyone comes to earth with a life purpose: we are here to experience, to learn, and to express ourselves based on that purpose. Whether we are working with the diseases of somatization or the psychic imbalances caused by the unexamined Other, shadow work helps us achieve our mission. We make sense of our experiences by learning from them, and the creative freedom that is released allows us to find our full expression.

Shadow work helps us align the wants of the personality with the needs of the Higher Self—shadow work is soul work. It works in gentle, yet powerful ways to change attitudes, awaken insight, and bring the strength and peace of acceptance. It gives us the capacity to move forward and "live the unlived life"; in other words, we learn to express our souls. But shadow work carries with it a price—to live the unlived life, we must have the pure intention of healing.

The Difference Between Hope and Intention

We often say, "I hope I can do this," or, "I hope I succeed." The word "hope" is vague and immeasurable and, as such, unattainable. Intent is clearly defined and can be visualized. When we say, "I intend to accomplish this," or "I intend to succeed," there is an accompanying mental picture of what steps will achieve the result. Intention is a word of power and action, essential to healing. With intention, we take a stance of responsibility and formulate action steps to achieve a desired result. It has nothing to do with wishful thinking. It is goal-directed and action-oriented. Pure intention is power, responsibility, commitment, and magic.

The Healing Power of Pure Intention

Prayer is one of the few forms of pure intention. When we engage in prayer, there is usually no ulterior motive and no need for defense mechanisms. During the act of prayer, we communicate directly with our Spiritual Source so there is little need for self-deception. The request, thanks, or intent is moving away from the ego-self into a greater dimension and greater purpose.

In your shadow work, you should not concern yourself with proper nouns. Your Spiritual Source is your Spiritual Source—call it any name you wish, be it God or Goddess, Tao . . . or nothing at all. What's important is that you call it. Prayer is a way to set up a connection to your Higher Self, ask for guidance, and attune yourself to your soul's purpose.

If prayer makes you uncomfortable, it could be because you grew up with the "I'm so bad I'm going straight to hell" form of prayer. This version is not a good way to ask for help. Short and sweet prayers work the best—no fancy words, just honesty and the pure intention of asking for help. During meditation, close your eyes, open your heart, and let the healing power of pure intention flow in. Guidance and support are available if you ask for it—learn to accept what the universe has to offer.

Linking with your Spiritual Source

We have explored the Higher Self several times in this book—that part of us which allows us to be clear, wise, and aware. It sees reality as it is and focuses on our potentials rather than our limiting beliefs. The Higher Self is a symbolic representation of the Spiritual Source that connects all of us. It is not "out there" somewhere; it dwells within and is not constrained by the human ways we try to explain it.

The concept of having a Higher Self within may be foreign to some of us. We are taught by our culture to look outside ourselves for wisdom. Overreliance on others—from clergy, mentors, and parents to psychologists, astrologers, and psychics—is disempowering.

Yes, we sometimes need temporary teachers and guides, but we forget we have all the answers we need about ourselves inside us—if we learn how to trust our inner knowledge.

To access your Higher Self/Spiritual Source directly, try this exercise (allow at least twenty minutes): Disconnect the phone and loosen any tight clothing. Light candles or do anything else that signals you are entering sacred space. It may be helpful to tape-record this exercise and play it back as you visualize.

As with all activities in this book, ground, center, and cast the circle of protection. At the very least, bring your attention to your breathing and heart area. Take slow, deep breaths until you feel yourself relax. Close your eyes—as you inhale, breathe in a beautiful light from above. Make it a color that speaks to you of universal love and acceptance. Rose pink is a good place to start, but allow this warm light to be any color you choose.

Feel loved and protected. Say out loud: "I am open to my highest awareness and will listen carefully to my inner voice. I receive guidance and protection at all times." If you find your mind wandering, gently bring it back to your deep breathing.

When you are relaxed and centered, imagine yourself to be in an art gallery. You are surrounded by beautiful works of art. You have never seen anything like it before. Everywhere you look, there is a stunning painting or piece of sculpture. You have read of such places but didn't know until this moment that they really existed. Stroll the hallways and breathe in the magnificence. Time stands still in this place of splendor.

There, in front of you, stands the most radiant sculpture you have ever seen. You can't take your eyes off of it. It draws you closer and closer. As you approach, you are amazed because it is a likeness of you. Everything about this figure is soul-perfect. You realize it is sentient and wants to talk with you. Your heart opens wider as you understand what you are looking at—this transcendent work of art is your Higher Self.

What do you see? Describe the sculpture in detail. Use whatever details (male, female, human, animal, angel, color, light, young, or old) that lead you to believe this work of art has access to the ultimate truths about you. It knows all about the universe, your place in it, and your purpose here on earth.

Make a list of questions you want to ask. There are no limits—you can ask this image absolutely anything. Have a conversation with your Higher Self and record the dialogue in writing. You might ask, "What is my mission?" or, "What work must I do to fully express what I have to offer?" Take your time with this. Trust what you hear.

After awhile, the sculpture merges with you and the two of you become as one. The access to the ultimate truths about your life now resides within you. As your Higher Self melts into the core of your being, it whispers to you, "Thank you. I am _____." What secret does your Higher Self reveal to you? You now have a relationship with the Higher Self and Spiritual Source. The word "relationship" implies a communication between two individuals (not necessarily people). You need guidance and support to find your life path: What does your Higher Self need from you?

Stay with the feeling of union for a few moments. Know that this loving Higher Self is available to you at any time, in any place. All you have to do is ask for its help. Slowly bring your consciousness back to breathing and the current surroundings. Place the palms of your hands on the floor to ground yourself. Stretch. Move around. Eat a snack.

When you feel yourself to be in a fully conscious state, examine what your Higher Self told you. What guidance did it offer? Did it speak to you concretely or in metaphor? What images or words did you receive? Are there several possible interpretations to what it said? What new insights do you have about the direction of your life and its overall meaning?

We experience, learn, and express. What did you experience? What did you learn? How can making conscious contact with your Spiritual Source assist you in expressing your soul? What is the most useful thing you discovered in this dialogue? What still seems unclear for you? Is trust an issue? Do you trust that you will receive guidance and protection if you ask for it? Why or why not? If you find that trusting anyone or anything is difficult for you, meditate with the Fool (0) as a tarot card focus. How do you react to the phrases "trust the process" and "leap of faith"? Make an entry in your journal.

So far, you have encountered the shadow and found gifts in the dark. You have met your Higher Self and recognized it as a work of art and wellspring for guidance. Perhaps you are taking baby-steps towards trusting your inner wisdom. It's time for an alchemy of integrating fragments; the healing begins with you.

The Nature of Healing

The root word for "heal" is derived from a Middle English word *hal*, meaning "to make whole."[1] Healing can be defined as the integration of body, mind, and spirit. The tradition of healing is ancient. Primitive people knew intuitively that healing was to make whole. Their attitudes and behaviors served as the basis for healing and was grounded in the feminine aspects of nurturance, intuition, and empathy.[2]

Healing occurs in a variety of ways, and the exact mechanism is unknown. Some believe it is primarily spiritual, while others reject the notion of spirituality. No matter what our opinions are, each of us has the capacity to become a healer when we recognize our own feelings, thoughts, and behaviors. All body systems are affected by how we think, what we eat, how we behave, and the choices we make. When we recognize and acknowledge our body-mind connection, we can begin to awaken the healer within.

We evolve as healers when we participate in our own healing through relationships and attunement to our inner wisdom. As we move closer to a higher consciousness, we become more involved with healing and the growth process at all levels: physical, mental, emotional, psychological, and spiritual. As Jung would say, we "find our soul."

A primary way we can develop into healers is to have firsthand experience in healing our own pain. As we have seen so far, the shadow can be physical or emotional pain, broken relationships or spiritual unrest. Whatever it is, it must be faced before we can become healers. We cannot become whole until we have faced the whole.

At some point we must address the shadow and examine our own wounds. We need to examine our weaknesses, as well as recognize and develop our strengths (the Bright Shadow). It is only when we face and integrate the shadow that we allow a powerful healing dimension to be born. Without healing, or channeling our wounds into healing conduits, there is little chance of emerging with the strength to heal others.

The Wounded Healer

At one time or another, in one way or another, each of us has been wounded. Wounding takes many forms and has many faces. For some, it may be a traumatic physical wound; for others, child abuse, rape, physical and emotional abuse, death of a loved one, or abandonment. Wounded-ness is not always obvious. Some of us use our open wounds to help another—an example would be a still active alcoholic working as a counselor on a drug rehabilitation unit. In seeking to help others they unconsciously look for ways to help themselves. Healers working through the defense mechanism of projection (see chapter 5) are actually trying to help themselves as they project healing energies onto others.[3]

Before we embark on the journey of healing others, we must first heal our own wounds and nurture our own strengths. Without facing our own individual wounds, we will unintentionally project our hurts onto another.

Self-healing is a lifelong process. Just because we emerge healed from one crisis does not mean we have completed our soul work. As long as we live, we will continue to have unexpected challenges and opportunities to develop wisdom. It is through our ongoing conscious awareness of personal pain that we can learn compassion, forgiveness, and love.

It is never too late to heal an old trauma. During times of emotional wounding, we often give our power to another. We become stronger when we learn to reclaim our power of personal choice. The greatest source of power is from within and from attunement with the channel of healing available to us from higher guidance. When we connect "above and below," we are on the ever-upward spiral of healing: the meaning of wounds become clear and life starts to make sense.

Discovering the Light Within

Many years ago, I concluded that we are not human beings attempting to be spiritual, but spiritual beings trying to be human. The term "spirit" comes to the English-speaking world from several sources: in Latin, the term was derived from *spiritus*, "breath." Ancient Greeks evolved the term from their word for "wind." Biblical texts describe it as the *ruach*, the breath of divinity flowing through us. Buddhists think of it as an inner light or source of truth. In modern times, we have come to view it as inner guidance or a higher power.[4]

The most important thing in defining spirit is the recognition that it is a essential to human nature, both physically and emotionally. This yearning varies from person to person, but it is present in us when we search for any type of meaning in our lives and try to make sense of it all. By now, some of you may have stopped reading this or are looking at it with a feeling of skepticism. That's fine—you are where you are and my truths are not your truths. I am proposing that the act of searching is itself a spiritual act. This yearning for "something more," or looking for the "unlived life" is proof we are spiritual beings.

Spirit is experienced when we turn inward to explore the human capacity for love, caring, honesty, compassion, wisdom, creativity, and imagination. No clashing thunder or bolts of lightning are required; it is simply the conscious seeking of light, truth, and connection with the Spiritual Source in whatever manner we choose. This conscious search is the essence of a spiritual journey.

Yes, some people do embark on a spiritual journey with crashes of thunder, but not all travellers start the trip with lofty ideals. Many of us begin the journey while in the midst of life's shadows. We are the ones who live in "the dark night of the soul," wrestling with the "winter of our discontent."

My spiritual journey began in 1983, in the bottom of a bottle. I was at the end of the road with nowhere left to go. I bought my ticket with despair. So you see, pure motives are not a prerequisite for safe passage.

Regardless of the port of entry, all of us have the same opportunity. Each and everyone of us has the capacity to undertake the spiritual journey required for self-healing. There are no credentials, no requirements, and no prescribed paths. The only things necessary are an open mind and heart and the willingness to take risks and explore.

One who makes a spiritual journey is never the same: she leads a life of loving usefulness. She has found meaning in her life and has a sense of purpose. The reward for the search is coming to understand why we are here and what our mission is on earth.

A Time for Healing

In chapter 2, you performed the "Healing Heart" meditation. Take a moment to review it. The heart is where all healing happens. As with other activities in this book, ground, center, and cast the circle of protection. Lie down comfortably or sit in your meditation position. Slow your breathing. Inhale and exhale deeply. Allow your whole body to relax. Say out loud: "Love heals me and sets my spirit free."

When you are ready, picture above you a radiant white light. Draw this beautiful light into you with each full breath and allow it to rest in your heart area. Feel it filling you with the warm glow of pure love and acceptance. This light is all-forgiving and as it extends outward from your heart, it turns a magnificent shade of rose pink, the color of universal love. Feel the light spreading throughout your body in a warm glow, filling your heart with unconditional acceptance.

Ask for healing to be sent to you in whatever way is appropriate. Remain as open and relaxed as possible so that you can experience whatever form the healing might take.

Rest in the light's peace until you feel lighter and completely calm.

When you feel the healing is over, give thanks and say something like this: "I thank the Source for the experience of healing"—your own words work best in this exercise. Breathe more deeply and gradually become aware of your surroundings. Once your attention is back to the room, open your eyes and ground yourself by placing the palms of both hands on the floor. Move your feet and wiggle your toes to confirm groundedness. Make an entry in your journal.

How did you feel before and after the exercise? What was the difference, if anything? Did you feel a sense of forgiveness of yourself? Why or why not? Are you more connected to the flow of spirit? How can this feeling help you with shadow work, or can it? Why or why not? Know that the light within you shines and is available at any time, in any place. All you need to do is ask.

The Star of Illumination—
The Healing Begins with You

Appendix A divides the cards into the challenges and gifts of the shadow. The challenges describe the feeling or thinking state when you are unaware of the shadow operating within you. The gifts of the shadow depict the healing energy that is released through awareness, acceptance, the power of choice and contact with the Higher Self. In the Star of Illumination layout, you will find yourself working with the gifts of the shadow.

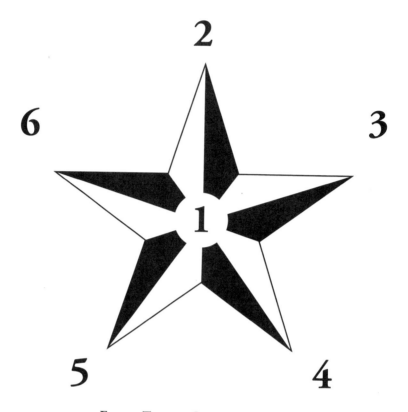

FIGURE THREE—STAR OF ILLUMINATION

Begin your tarot shadow work session by grounding, centering, and casting the circle of protection. At the very least, disconnect the phone and take slow, deep breaths to achieve a state of relaxation. Repeat the shadow work affirmation: "By embracing my dark shadows, I am healing and becoming whole. I am gaining wisdom and learning compassion." Because the focus of this layout is ways to begin the healing process, add to the affirmation: "I acknowledge that all my past experiences have brought me to this moment of acceptance. I love myself just as I am. My power rests in being who I am."

Star of Illumination Spread:
The Healing Begins with You

Position One—The Empty Vessel: What needs to be healed? Place one of the shadow cards from your original Star of Discovery spread (chapter 3) in position one. This is the focus and represents the area that is ready to be filled with light and healed. Shuffle the remaining twenty-one cards, including any you have out on your altar. Concentrate on what the shadow needs in order to be illuminated. When you are ready, randomly select five cards face-down. Place them face-up in positions two through six, as shown in the illustration. Look at the entire layout and record your initial reaction to it in the journal. First impressions are usually accurate. Does it surprise you? Why or why not?

Position Two—The Beginning: What will begin the healing process of (Card 1)? What will begin the integration of this shadow? You may start to notice a change in the nuance of the card. For example, if you choose the card that represents anxiety/fear for position one and you drew the Star (17) for position two, you might interpret it by using the gifts of shadow: contacting your Spiritual Source will begin to heal your fear. A concrete action you could take toward this insight is learning how to meditate. Please refer to Appendix A.

Position Three—Formation: What will shape or give form to the healing process of (Card 1)? What will shape the integration of the shadow? Let's say you chose the card symbolizing denial of talents and abilities as the focus for this layout. Now you have drawn the Magician (1) for position three. In this example, you would use the gift of shadow work with the Magician: unexpressed talents and abilities may find their expression if you make a conscious choice and take appropriate action rather than simply wishing for success or fulfillment. We will explore how to create goals in the next section.

Note: This is only an example to get you started. Trust your inner wisdom and follow your intuition when working with any tarot layout.

Position Four—The Center: What is at the center or central to the healing process of _____ (Card 1)? What is at the center of integrating this shadow? Imagine you chose the card signifying low self-esteem (feelings of inferiority) as the focus. You find the Wheel of Fortune (10) in position four. You can interpret the answer using the gifts of shadow work: Central to integrating the shadow of low self-esteem is the need to determine how past events are affecting your present attitudes and behaviors. Appropriate actions central to the healing of low self-esteem would include: keeping a dream journal, working with tarot, being committed to journaling, or engaging in professional counseling to explore your past.

Position Five—The Need: What is needed for (Card 1) to heal? What is necessary for integration of this shadow? If you chose the card representing fear as the focus of this layout (position one), let's pretend Justice (11) shows up here in position five. Using the gifts of shadow work, you need to consider how resolving or releasing feelings from the past can help you integrate the shadow of fear. Chapter 7 offers a Mourning Rite for putting closure on a painful past. Chapter 8 looks at ways to move forward from the past without fear.

Position Six—The Gift: What gift of healing will you receive as a result of your work with (Card 1)? What gift will integration of this shadow give you? This is not as obvious as it may appear. You are the star and author of your own life; and recipient of the gifts of shadow work. No book can define and give meaning to your life. The healing energy that is released as the result of shadow work is yours to use as you see fit. Don't get stuck in the meanings of the cards given in Appendix A, because they will end up being too limiting. I cannot begin to imagine your full potential or how you will use the healing energy. You must choose how high you will soar. If you need a flying lesson, Appendix A can give you a boost to get you started but your take-off is limited only by your commitment to it. The power surges are up to you.

Here's an example: In the Star of Discovery spread (chapter 3), let's say the Chariot (7) appeared in position six, self-loathing. After meditation, you decided that it meant one of the reasons you are your own worst enemy (and therefore a victim) is due to a lack of direction in your life—and you sometimes act irresponsibly because of it. Now you have made a commitment to shake the victim archetype. You will define your goals and create a plan for change. The gift of integrating the Chariot's shadow may be twofold; you discover in your journey that there are past issues that need to be resolved before you can charge ahead. One of these issues is the realization of your aggressive drives. You tried so hard to kill them that you became a victim in your own life. By doing shadow work, you have learned to accept your aggressive nature and are learning to direct this drive into appropriate action. Great . . . but here's where the descriptions in Appendix A are too limiting. It's up to you to decide what "appropriate action" entails: Does it mean you take a vigorous exercise class to channel the energy? Will you join an activist group and become an organizer? Will you change jobs and look for a position of leadership in a competitive market? Only you can determine what is the right path to take. Use Appendix A to start your engine and get off the ground, always remembering the flight pattern is yours to make.

Make an entry in your journal about this entire spread. If you wish, photocopy the illustration for later reference. Save your insights because you will use them again when you create realistic goals for change at the end of the chapter. Leave the Star of Illumination layout on the shadow altar for awhile.

Incubate a dream about it (see chapter 5) or meditate with one of the cards as a focus. Contact the wisdom of your Higher Self. Encounter the Dark Goddess to see if she can help you put the information in perspective. Use all the skills you've learned so far to determine the significance of the Star of Illumination layout. If you gain new insights into the meaning of the cards over time, include those in your journal. Be sure to date all entries. Shadow work can be exhausting; take a break, play, and come back with a refreshed perspective. Celebrate your courage to change.

Seeing Change in Your Mind's Eye

The mind is good at thinking up negative scenarios and the results are usually negative. When the same power is harnessed to a positive goal, you can use your ability to visualize and create a positive future. Many of us are unconscious of the fact we image all the time. The pictures we project and the words we say combine to create our reality. Our images are so powerful that they create our future. Think about how contagious low morale is in the work place; if we moan and complain loud enough and long enough—sure enough—it's a terrible place to work. That's the power of projecting negative thought until it becomes our reality.

When we become conscious of the imaging process we can develop the ability to mold and shape our thoughts into a healthful, positive destiny. So powerful is imagery that we can use it to focus on problems and reframe negative past experiences in a more positive way. Reframing an event through imagery can allow us to let go of troubling thoughts and feelings that block healing.[5]

The purpose of some visualizations is to relax the mind by imaging a place of peace and harmony in your mind's eye. The second form of visualization is to create a situation where you can obtain information, reassurance, get help in problem-solving, and receive answers to important questions. This second type is known as creative visualization or creative imagery. It is useful to distinguish between the two: one is a technique for relaxation, and the other a method of linking with your inner guidance.[6]

As you can see, we are using both types of visualization techniques throughout this book; sometimes for relaxation, sometimes to tap your inner wisdom. Please remember that the inner guidance is best obtained in a state of relaxation. Imagery and relaxation are complementary strategies; by quieting the mind through focused attention you are in a receptive state to receive guidance.

The remainder of this work book focuses on molding and shaping thoughts into a healthful and positive destiny by problem-solving, reframing negative past experiences, and contacting inner wisdom through creative visualization. You have been doing this all along—now you are aware of the process.

We have been using creative imagery to concentrate on the past. It's time to harness that same power for a peek into the possible future. We create who we are. Try this activity to begin understanding the power of words and imagery: Take a piece of paper and begin writing: "I am . . ." Look at the clock and note the time. When you have breathed deeply and feel relaxed, begin filling in the sentence. "I am . . ." Do not take your pen off the page for ten minutes (this is important). Write continuously for ten solid minutes. Write everything that comes into your mind, even if it's "I am sooo tired" or "I am not going to get anything out of this stupid exercise." Stop at the end of ten minutes and read out loud what you wrote. You will be amazed at how much of your reality you have created with the power of your words. Now imagine how much you could accomplish if you spent ten minutes writing wonderful things about yourself and your life.

Try this: Go back to chapter 3 and reread the "Encountering the Dark Goddess" meditation. This time, make out a list of specific questions for her, things that are bothering you right now. Do the meditation again, but ask for guidance based on your list of questions. After you are relaxed, and before you enter the Crone's forest, say out loud: "I channel my highest good to transform my life. I am happy to be still and listen to my inner voice. I heal and grow every day." Can you hear the power of pure intention in these words? Notice how weak this sounds when said out loud: "I hope to transform my life, I hope to hear my inner voice, I hope I heal." Action words direct power. Make an entry in your journal and compare it with the one you made originally in chapter three. How is the encounter with the Dark Goddess different when you have a specific goal in mind as you visualize? Focused intention equals change and responsible, personal power.

Think Big, Act Small

You are lost the moment you know what the result will be.
Juan Gris

The Star of Illumination layout yielded a lot of information about how to integrate the shadow and let the healing begin. By now, your head may be swimming with insights, goals, plans, and ideas. But what to do with all the information? Good books are available about goal setting and making plans. Please refer to Appendix C for suggestions.

As you look at the Star of Illumination spread, ask yourself: How much do I want to do right now? What is my priority? What needs to be healed first? What is the most loving thing I can do for myself today? In three months? Six months? A year? What one thing do I need to do this very day to start the process of healing? Do I need to make a phone call? Contact a support group? Write a letter? Redo my résumé? Sign up for a class? Call a health professional or trusted counselor? Practice meditation? Keep a journal? Decide what part of the healing process must begin right now and what parts can wait.

Then be content that you exercised your power of choice and took action in your own behalf. After you make that call, contact a support group, write that letter, redo your résumé, or make an appointment to see someone, the next course of action will become apparent to you. By taking tiny steps through your power of choice, you have set in motion a powerful healing energy that feeds on your actions. Healing is exercising your spiritual muscles: the more you take small, healing steps on a daily basis, the stronger the healing force becomes.

A popular saying goes something like this: "Life is what happened to me while I was busy making other plans." It's good to have a sense of the "big picture," to have a direction, to know where your life is going, but the truth is we get to our destiny one day at a time. Goal setting and making plans are fine, but it is in the minutia that miracles occur. If we focus on the end result too much, the opportunities of the present moment pass us by. We may not know what is truly for our Highest Good. When you make a request to your Spiritual Source, add: "It's equivalent or better." If we are open and receptive to unexpected possibilities, the universe can surprise us with something beyond our wildest imaginings. In the true paradox of shadow work, when we let go of the need to control outcomes we find our personal power.

Staying in the past blocks healing and growth. Worrying about the wreckage of the future takes away precious energy that could be spent on doing what needs to be done today. So think big—set goals, make plans, expect good results—but act small . . . by taking loving care of ourselves each and every day, the future unfolds and takes care of itself.

This chapter has been about the work you do to heal yourself. In the next chapter, we will explore the work required to heal relationships. The healing journey requires that you pack lightly for the trip. Excess baggage may still be weighing you down. As we continue our shadow work, removing some of that baggage will become our focus.

Endnotes

1. Berube, Margery S., editor. *The American Heritage Dictionary*, Second College Edition, (Boston, Houghton Mifflin Company, 1985), p. 599

2. Noble, Vicki. *Making Ritual with Motherpeace Cards*. (New York, Three Rivers Press, Random House, 1998), pp. 77–79

3. Hover-Kramer, Dorthea, Ed.D., RN. *Healing Touch: A Resource for Health Care Professionals*. (Albany, New York, Delmar Publishers, 1996), pp. 221–222

4. Keegan, Lynn, Ph.D., RN. *The Nurse as Healer*. (Albany, New York, Delmar Publishers, 1994), p. 42

5. Roach, Sally and Beatrice Nieto, RN, MSN. *Healing and the Grief Process*. (Albany, New York, Delmar Publishers, 1997), p. 194

6. Angelo, Jack. *Hands-On Healing*. (Rochester, Vermont, Healing Arts Press, 1997), p. 124

Chapter 7

COMPASSION: THE INNER LIGHT

Where love rules, there is no rule to power; and where power dominates,
there love is lacking. The one is the shadow of the other.
C. G. Jung

THE GOAL IN THIS CHAPTER IS LEARNING FORGIVENESS OF OTHERS
through compassion. Forgiveness does not mean condoning or accepting hurtful behavior, but it does involve letting go of what happened in
the past. Forgiveness cannot be forced, but once achieved, offers tremendous personal freedom and a surge of creative energy.

We begin by considering the role of compassion in healing. Guided
activities are designed to help you examine areas of resentment, anger
and sadness; and to open the door for healing relationships. Once the
wounds are identified, creative visualization techniques help you let go
of them and move on. The focus throughout is claiming the pain of the
past and releasing it through the power of choice. The chapter concludes
with an opportunity to "Wish Upon a Star" for outward expression of
the inner light.

Compassion Is Not Pity

Compassion is often regarded as a type of sentimental pity towards those less fortunate than us—the sick, the poor, the mentally ill. This kind of thinking taints compassion with the sour odor of superiority. Such pity is condescension and is applied to emphasize the differences between "us and them."

The root word of compassion is the Latin *cum patior*, meaning "to suffer with" or be passionate for someone else's well-being.[1] Compassion is more than the simple act of caring. It leads us to go where it hurts, to enter places of pain and to share in brokenness, fear, and confusion. Compassion means full immersion in the condition of being human.

Compassion is not a mere quiet sympathy with others because compassion always requires action. We no longer give help because we are supposed to, or give aid with the expectation of getting something in return. We do not forgive because it shows how "evolved" we are, but because it's the compassionate thing to do. To discover for yourself if you engage in pity or true compassion, ask this question: When I help another, does it make me feel superior or humble?

Compassion is located in the heart, the place of our soul, inner guidance, and healing. The more hurts we've encountered, the more potential we have to be compassionate. As we seek to embrace our shadow and open up, healing energy is released. When we begin the process of self-healing and discover our light within, we begin to understand people and events in a new way. What once baffled us now starts to make sense and allows us an outward expression of the inner light.

Forgive or Forget It

Forgiveness does not mean condoning hurtful or ignorant behavior, but it does involve letting go of the past. An unwillingness to forgive attaches us all the more to our pain. Hatred saps energy and allows us to be controlled by another. As long as we direct our anger, or shadow, to those who have hurt us, they still hold our attention and power.

One of the most powerful aspects of our humanness is how we continue to carry the burdens of our wounds. We hear statements such as, "I will never trust another man as long as I live after what he did to me," or, "My childhood was so horrible, I've been messed up ever since. I'll never be happy because of it." Attitudes like these condemn us to a lifetime of pain and suffering and cry out for the need to forgive. When we stubbornly hang onto our pain, we block our possibility of finding happiness.

Forgiveness is power; it is not a weak or passive act. The act of forgiveness cannot be forced, but once achieved, offers personal freedom. When we forgive, we take back our power; and real healing begins because it allows us to become free of others. We move out of the past and into the present moment where blocks can be dissolved and healing energy released. The act of forgiveness will not change the past, but it will assuredly change us—and the possible future—forever.

To make a shift from the chronic wounding of the ego into the spirit's place of healing, try this affirmation: "I release all negative feelings that hold me back from being happy and free. I forgive the past and live in the here and now." Say it out loud daily, even if you don't believe a word of it. Because of the power of words, change will occur.

The Power of Choice

A popular twelve-step program has a slogan that says change will occur when we're "sick and tired of being sick and tired." Or, put another way, when the pain of staying the same exceeds the pain of change, change will occur. We have the power to change our attitudes and beliefs whenever we honor our own spiritual potential and realize we are worthy of change. One way to affirm ourselves is to examine our attitudes, feelings, and beliefs, and change what is no longer useful through the power of choice.

Throughout the course of shadow work, and especially in this chapter, look at any anger or hatred you still cling to and ask: How does anger or hatred benefit me? What is my "payback" for hanging on to rage? How do these feelings help me grow? What is the value of giving my power to another? What is the reward of being a victim? You may find yourself hard-pressed to come up with a solid answer to any of these questions.

We can learn and grow from our painful experiences or we can stay locked in the shadows of blame and shame. We can learn compassion for those that suffer as we do, or our attitudes can turn us into mental cripples. We are the authors of our own lives. The choice is ours and ours alone to make.

Engaging in shadow work is one choice among many. It's not the path for everyone. The journey to freedom has a multitude of roads. It doesn't matter which route you select—but it's important that you choose one. The process of healing begins when you become willing to exercise your power of choice. Try this affirmation: "I am capable of healing my life. I choose to seek help when I feel it will benefit my growth."

Pick a Pain—Any Pain

A little store near me sells small meditation stones with various words engraved in them: words like courage, gratitude, believe, kindness, wonder, forgive, expect miracles, magic, Goddess. They are placed around the home or office to remind us to practice that word or hold that quality in our everyday lives. These trinkets sold very well—all except the "forgive" stones. The owner couldn't sell them, even at half-price. She told me that either very few people had anything to forgive (which she found hard to believe); or, very few people wanted to be reminded of the need to forgive.

Forgiveness has nothing to do with accepting hurtful behavior. It's not about inviting someone we have forgiven back into our life or keeping them out. It is an attitude that sets us free so we aren't continually victimized by our wounds. We forgive because it is the loving thing to do for us.

Here's the tricky part. We can't force something to go away by pretending it didn't happen (that's called denial). Before we can let go of a painful experience, we must first examine it. We need to claim ownership of the wound before we can move on. Begin this activity with an affirmation of truth: "I am entitled to speak from my heart and express my feelings. I am developing integrity every time I speak my truth."

You are going to make a list of everyone who has hurt you, no matter when, where or how. Large, small, or in between—if you are holding a grudge, for whatever reason, that person or event belongs on the list. Be specific as to time, place, what happened, why this hurt you. You want to put as much detail into this as possible.

It's important to write down your feelings at the time it happened, your feelings about it now and why you think you are still hanging on to the pain. Be nasty—don't take the other person's side. This is your list in your confidential journal. If you think you need to be profane, be profane. No one else is going to see it. The idea is to let all the stuffed feelings pour out. Do not censor your writing in any way. If you try to be "polite," or worse, "nice," you will render this exercise useless. Absolute honesty about your feelings is required here. You will gain nothing by hiding from your truth.

Now spend some time reading through the lists. In a nonjudgmental way, acknowledge that this is how you feel, or felt, at the time. As you read the list, say out loud: "Events from the past have no power to hurt me today. I am safe and protected at all times." Take each item on your list and place it in one of the following categories on a separate sheet of paper:

* needs reparation

* needs forgiveness (ugh, there's that word again)

* needs mourning

* the gifts that hide in the dark

This would include valuable learning experiences and anything you can turn into a goal for the future. For example, if you suffered an abusive relationship, you can take that experience and volunteer at a battered women's shelter.

If you find yourself having trouble getting started because, after all, nice girls don't get mad, go back to the original Star of Discovery tarot layout in chapter 3. The pain from the past is hidden in the shadow. It may help you begin to identify the source of your wounding. Save the list—you will use it for several activities in this chapter.

Resentment Means to "Re-feel"

Unresolved anger saps energy by the very strength it needs to stay suppressed. It can lie at the heart of depression, addiction, and physical distress. Resentment literally means to "re-feel" or "feel again." If you are suffering from unresolved anger which has festered into a resentment, it is likely you are suffering from physical symptoms as well.

Resentment may be noticed as a vague, uncomfortable thought, something "eating away at you," a tightness in your abdomen or a feeling of not being able to get enough air. Regardless of how the resentment is experienced, it represents unfinished business and needs attention. Anger is at the heart of resentment and can be the key to discovering the changes you need to make for healing to begin. Letting go of resentment is not a passive act and requires a conscious choice and action on your part.

You probably listed family members, ex-spouses, ex-bosses, and former lovers on your list from the previous section. Perhaps you have unaddressed resentments about a current relationship, too. One method to get rid of these resentments is to write an unposted letter to the person, regardless of whether the person is alive or dead. The purpose is not to send the letter, but to express your feelings about the situation.

At the beginning of the book, the shadow was defined as unresolved inner conflicts and unexpressed emotions. If we believe we can't resent a person (or be angry at him because it isn't "proper"), then the unexpressed emotions will surface as shadows or, the shadows may be turned inward in the form of depression, illness, and accidents. The next activity will help you find a voice for your unexpressed emotions—at last.

Dear John—
Writing the Unsent Letter

Writing unposted letters to people who have hurt us—alive or dead—can be liberating. By knowing we are not going to send the letter, we have complete freedom to say anything we want in any language we want. By not mailing the letter, we cannot hurt another or fear retaliation. This is a safe expression for raw emotions. Venting the anger and/or resentments will free the energy we've wasted on trying to keep our emotions out of awareness and under control.

Word of caution here: You are writing letters to people who have hurt you to put closure on the wound, or at least, move in the direction of closure. Do not write a letter to open an old wound or wallow around in the pain. Going over and over a particular incident only serves to get you stuck in the past. The wound becomes the defining characteristic of your life when you are in the "replay" mode. Staying stuck gives power to the problem. Letter writing should be a means of letting go, not a method of bringing up bitterness over and over again. The whole idea of letter writing is to rid yourself of a resentment so you can focus on solutions and move forward with your life.

Begin your unsent letter writing project with this affirmation, or better yet, make up your own: "By venting my resentments and claiming my pain in this safe way, I liberate myself from a wounded past. I have the power to remove myself from all negative situations which harm me." Make an entry in your journal about how you feel right this moment as you commence to write a letter. Righteous indignation? Anger? Rage? Condescension? What do you hope to gain? Be honest and record the feelings.

From the list in the previous section, pick a pain—any pain, choose a "recipient" for your letter. Remember, you are not going to send it and the person does not have to be alive. In the letter, clearly state what happened, why it hurt you, and how you felt about it then. Describe the ways this wound has had a lasting effect on your life. What have you missed because of it? State how you feel about it now. Don't censor your writing or worry about being polite. Use powerful language and say everything you need to say to this person.

When you can write no more, read the letter out loud to yourself as though you were actually addressing the person face to face. Put as much anger and hurt into the reading as you truly feel. After you have done this, take a moment to repeat the affirmation above. Breathe deeply to bring you back to a state of calm. Make another entry in your journal: Do you feel differently, now that you have found a safe voice for unexpressed emotions? How? Save the letter because you will use it again when you perform a mourning ritual.

Dance with Your Anger

Freeing yourself from old anger can dramatically improve your health: ulcers may heal, high blood pressure may resolve itself, addictive behavior may stop. One of the most liberating forms of anger reduction is physical exercise. (Please check with a health professional before engaging in this activity.) As you begin, say out loud: "I have the right to be angry." Read one of your angry letters again to get yourself in the mood.

Select angry music, preferably without lyrics. If you don't know what angry music is, choose a piece that is lively, with a prominent drum beat. Close the shades if you are self-conscious about dancing. When the music starts, begin by just listening to it as you visualize your anger. Then tap your fingers or feet in time to the music. Allow your body to sway. Feel your anger becoming stronger. If you feel like humming, chanting, or screaming, do so. As you feel yourself getting more involved with the music, begin to move around. Don't think about what you are doing—this is not an Arthur Murray dance class. Concentrate on the feeling and let anger be your choreographer. Continue dancing until the music stops or you are fatigued.

As with any physical activity, you will need a cool-down period. When the music is over, continue walking around the room for a few minutes. As your breathing returns to normal, make an entry in your journal. What was it like to dance with your anger? Did it help? Why or why not? Do you feel lighter now? Less angry?

After you have made an entry, sit quietly and breathe in a slow deep way until you feel calm and relaxed. Drink a glass of water or juice to rehydrate yourself after exercise. Know that you have just learned to vent your anger in a safe, no-one-gets-hurt manner. Dance with your anger whenever you feel its power start to overtake you. It is a constructive method of letting go of an emotion that can kill you.

So Much Loss, So Much Pain

Death. Nobody likes to say the word in this culture. But the truth is people die and we are left to pick up the pieces. Some of us have unfinished business with the deceased: regrets, anger, pain. A gap is left when someone dies, regardless of the quality of the relationship. We can have feelings of rage, despair, loss, or sadness.

Even if we have had no direct contact with death, we may still need to deal with the consequences of loss. All change involves loss. We experience loss not only with death of a loved one, or a pet, but with events like changing career, divorce, marriage (loss of the single life), or moving to a new home. Some of us grieve over lost childhood or loss of menstruation at menopause. We may grieve over the loss of a body part after surgery, especially related to cancer; or loss of financial freedom when our circumstances change. In early recovery, it is common to grieve the loss of alcohol and drugs.

Very often, our situations reflect a whole pattern of loss which has gone on throughout life. Make yourself comfortable and relax the body by deep breathing. Look back over your life and make a careful list of all your losses. Include things like losing friendships, missing an opportunity, and misplacing treasured items. All perceived losses belong on your list. Take your time and notice any feelings generated by a particular loss: grief, sadness, anger, despair, regret, etc. What strategies did you develop to cope and integrate the loss into your life as you moved forward? For instance, if you suffered the death of your partner due to AIDS, what did you do to recover? Did you need a period of isolation to discover your own inner strengths? What was the direct consequence and result of that particular loss? With any loss, you can at least write that you experienced the pain and survived. Perhaps you gained compassion for those who are in the same situation. What were the unexpected benefits of a loss? For example, if you lost your job, did you find a new career? If your life partner died, did you find a strength and creativity you didn't know you possessed?

When you have not been able to integrate a loss into your life, you have probably felt the painful shadows of its stored energies; an example is the use of alcohol as a primary coping strategy. Try this exercise to begin healing a lifetime of loss. After you have relaxed your whole body by through deep breathing, say out loud: "I have survived loss and am stronger for it. I release the pain of loss, doubt, and fear. I choose to live my life fully. Love heals me and sets my spirit free."

As you take deep breaths, locate the feeling of loss in your body. It may be in your heart, around your womb, or at the site of surgery. Continue slow breathing and focus on this body part to feel the loss. Let your inner vision reveal the circumstances of the loss to you. Cry if you feel like it because tears wash the soul. When you have a clear picture of the situation, imagine a radiant purple light above your head. As you inhale, bring this light into your heart. As you exhale, allow the light of profound healing to go directly to the feeling of loss in your body. Feel it permeate every cell. Using the power of pure intention, ask out loud for healing of the loss. Listen for the voice of inner wisdom to see if you are given guidance on what to do. Breathe in the healing light, breathe out the energies of the loss situation. Keep releasing this way until the loss is cleared from your body, or you begin to feel a sense of peace.

Once the feelings of loss have been reduced, continue to breathe in the healing purple light for a few moments. Say out loud: "I am grateful for this healing." Stay with this feeling as long as you like. When you are ready, open your eyes and become aware of your surroundings. Ground yourself by moving your feet or placing the palms of your hands on the floor. Make an entry in your journal.

If you are mourning a missing body part, you are not going to regenerate it during this exercise. The objective here is to gain insight, peace, and compassion, not cure symptoms. Insight and a new perspective will allow you to accept what cannot be changed and move forward in your life—with the courage to change the things you can.

Sometimes relationships or attitudes need healing. Think of the healing exercise as a visual affirmation. Creative imagery can be used to heal relationships, too. Perform the visualization above, but see, in your mind's eye, the situation that needs healing. Send purple light to it and use the power of pure intention. Realize you cannot change another against his will or without his permission, but you can send healing energy to the overall state of affairs. It is not up to you to determine how the healing energy will be used. By all means send it—then trust that things will work out for everyone's Highest Good, no matter how it turns out. When you send healing energy to a situation, say: "I send healing energy for the good of all, harm none, according to free will, its equivalent or better."

Healing Childhood

As children, we all have specific needs for food, shelter, love, approval, affection, and respect. Some children grow up in an atmosphere of violence, abuse, or neglect. Others have material needs met, but experience cold, distant parenting. Still others lose a parent to death, divorce, or abandonment. One of the most common patterns of loss in adulthood is unfulfilled childhood needs.

When we have this pattern of loss, we do not stop growing chronologically, but growth on the emotional level is interrupted. As adults, all further hurts reinforce this damaged concept we have of ourselves. We may live our lives filled with fear, confusion, anxiety, or anger. Emotional situations and relationships can trigger unconscious memories of childhood hurts and, as a result, we end up behaving in immature ways.

The following exercise will help you start the process of healing a painful childhood. From my personal experience, childhood hurts go the deepest and take the longest to heal. Seek the wisdom of a trusted friend or professional counselor if you need it. Take deep breaths and allow your whole body to relax. Say out loud: "I forgive the past and live in the here and now."

Think about painful memories from childhood. Do not trivialize them just because you are an adult. See the pain through the eyes and heart of the child you were at the time it happened. If you hear someone in your head shouting, "Oh, grow up!" it's your harsh inner parent. Tell him to be quiet. Focus on just one or two incidents at first and make an entry in your journal about each. Try to be as detailed as possible when describing a situation.

When you can write no more, answer the following questions: Did you notice anything about your body that changed as you wrote about a painful childhood memory? What was it? Did your heart rate or breathing pattern increase? Did you feel nauseated or start to perspire as you recalled childhood? Did the center of your chest or your throat feel tight? Did you feel yourself start to get angry or sad? If you answered yes to one of these questions, you may have unresolved childhood pain.

The following exercise is designed to start the healing of a specific childhood hurt. You will use one of the issues from the previous journal entry. Children are fragile, so it is important that you ground, center and cast the circle of protection for this activity. Your wounded child needs to feel safe. Light a pink candle and say out loud: "I am safe and protected at all times. I am capable of healing the past because I survived it. As I own my power, I release my pain and forgive the past. I love myself and I am free."*

---

* Never underestimate the power of words. Say words like these out loud, even if you don't believe them. Change will occur.

Look at the glowing pink candle. Breathe deeply and bring a rose pink light into your heart area. Feel yourself surrounded by rose pink light and unconditional love. Identify the issue which came up in the previous journal entry. State this out loud. Be specific. See yourself at the age you were when it happened. Locate in your body where you feel the issue and let that place be the focus. Rely on your inner vision more than adult memory. Ask the child that you see what she or he needs from you. Wait for a reply.

Carry out what your child tells you to do. If you get no response, do what you feel a child like this would need. A particular issue has come up because you are ready to let go of it. See the pain wrapped in white light, perhaps like a beautiful balloon. Take hold of the balloon filled with pain and gently let go of it. Say goodbye and tell yourself you no longer need this old energy.

There is now a space in you where the old pain used to be. Breathe in the loving rose pink light to fill the gap. Feel the void being replaced with a sense of peace. Say out loud: "Thank you for this healing." Come back in your own time. Gently open your eyes and return to your normal surroundings. Breathe deeper and move your feet. Place the palms of your hands on the floor to ground yourself.

When you are ready, make an entry in your journal. What did your child ask you to do? What does your child need from you as an adult? If you received no response from your child, what can you do to help this child in pain? Trust your inner wisdom because you know what is best for this child. It can be as simple as writing an unsent letter or as profound as making an appointment to see a counselor. Think of one concrete thing you can do for yourself—and do it today.

Love Means (Sometimes) Having to Say You're Sorry

Please excuse the mixed metaphors, but in the dance of anger it takes two to tango. The shadow isn't polite and it doesn't care who it hurts when it erupts. We do and say things we later regret when under its power. So far, we have looked at methods to recognize and embrace the shadow, locate areas of personal pain that need healing, and explore ways of letting go of the past. Before we can move on, we need to examine the manner in which we have hurt others and make amends where appropriate.

In the dual nature of shadow work, if we can give forgiveness, then we must be able to ask for it, too. Think of this as the "repair shop"; in the course of doing shadow work, we may find something hurtful that we have done and realize it needs reparation. Regret over the past can be debilitating to growth.

To effectively remove the emotional block of remorse, we need to make amends and move on. But there is a catch to asking for forgiveness or offering an apology: We must let go of any notion that the other person is obligated to accept the amend. The sole objective in making amends is to free us from the crippling emotion of guilt. We need to make reparation where appropriate, but the recipient does not have to accept the gesture.

When making amends, stick to your part in the situation, even if the party in question was a jerk. You are not offering an apology and a reminder of how hurtful the other person was to you. Keep your list of grievances for another time and place. If you bring an elephant's memory into your apology, you will put the recipient in a defensive posture and nothing can be repaired.

It may be enough to simply offer an apology to the person concerned, send some flowers, or mail a note. Short and sincere apologies work the best. Never beg for forgiveness because humility is not humiliation. You are a worthwhile human being and whether or not the other person accepts the amend is not your outcome to control.

Direct reparation is not always possible due to geography or death. In these circumstances, write a letter of apology to the person anyway. Use a photograph or mental picture as a connection to that person as you compose the note. Light a white candle as a symbol of clearing away the old regrets forever. Read the letter at the graveside, if appropriate, and leave a peace offering of flowers, especially white or pink carnations. You can also place the letter, candle, and flowers on your shadow altar for awhile.

Earlier in this chapter, you were asked to make a list and divide it into four categories. Look at it now and review your entry under "Needs

Repair." Begin this exercise by deep breathing to relax your whole body. Light a white candle and say out loud: "I acknowledge my mistakes and reaffirm my self-esteem. I am thankful for the learning experience which comes from making mistakes and will do what is best for me in the future."

On a sheet of paper, describe the act for which you wish forgiveness. Are you able to make direct amends or do you need to write an unposted letter? Are you ready to forgive yourself for this action? Are you prepared to receive forgiveness or rejection? Write a letter stating exactly how you feel now. Will you send the letter, read it at the graveside or place it on the shadow altar? Would it be better to make this apology face to face? Can you make an amend without mentioning the perceived character defects of the other person? Is it appropriate to send flowers? Do you need to make a phone call? Are you prepared for the possibility that making amends is a liberating experience? Once you make the amend, can you let go and move on? Do you need to discuss this with a trusted friend or counselor? List anything that you would like to do—and are prepared to do—by way of reparation. Set a date to do it—then do it.

Receiving Forgiveness

If we are willing to give forgiveness, we must be willing to receive it. If you are a woman, it is probably easier to give than to receive. Think for a moment how effortless it is to give someone a gift. Now recall how difficult it is to receive one. The same is true for receiving the gift of forgiveness.

Guided imagery is helpful in reprogramming your response to situations and releasing old emotional blocks. If you find it difficult to "see" an image, then you can act as if you do; it is the healing power of pure intention that counts. The following visualization will help you receive forgiveness, whether the other person can give it, or not. Look at your list under the heading "needs forgiveness." Recall a specific situation.

Light a pink or white candle and begin this exercise by relaxing your entire body through deep breathing. When you are relaxed, say out loud: "I receive forgiveness and feel spiritual peace because of it." Picture in your mind the person from whom you wish to receive forgiveness.

When you have a strong image of this person, read your letter of apology out loud. In your mind's eye, see the other person receiving it and responding to you in a loving way. If you have difficulty "seeing" this, verbalize the scenario that you desire. Tell the story of what you want to have happen in this situation. Say it out loud.

Ask the other person to forgive you, then imagine that forgiveness is given to you. Let yourself feel the forgiveness flowing to you and going directly into your heart. Allow the feeling of forgiveness to spread throughout your entire body in a warm glow.

Thank the person and make any gesture that seems appropriate — hugging, kissing, shaking hands, crying, laughing, etc. Allow that person to fade from your mind by sending them on their way with love. Notice how much lighter you feel now that you have received forgiveness.

When you are ready, slowly open your eyes and become aware of your surroundings. Breathe deeply, move your feet and touch the floor with your hands. Make an entry in your journal. What was it like to receive forgiveness? Be specific.

Moving On

The work in this chapter is about freeing yourself from the bonds which hold you forever in the past. These weighted burdens block the flow of healing energy and rob you of your creativity. By following the suggestions so far in this workbook, you are now ready to carry out a mourning ritual. Gather together any letters from the previous exercises that symbolize what you need to grieve. If you do not wish to burn the letters, make a list of things to mourn on another piece of paper. Pour your heart out. Include absolutely everything you feel sad about and also those things you wish to let go. Refer to the list you made earlier, under the category of "needs mourning."

Reread "Encountering the Dark Goddess" in chapter 2, for she is the Goddess of death and rebirth. Use black candles and objects on your shadow altar and burn a heavy incense such as vanilla, jasmine, opium, or narcissus. If you feel like dressing in black for this mourning rite, do so. Place the tarot card Death (13) on your altar to symbolize death of the old, and transformation.

Allow at least twenty minutes when you will be undisturbed for the mourning rite. Disconnect the phone and loosen any tight clothing. Place the letters or list on the altar and be sure to have a fireproof container handy. It can be an ashtray or baking dish, but make certain it isn't flammable. You will need matches or a lighter. It is important to ground, center, and cast the circle of protection for this ritual. If this feels wrong to you, at least say out loud: "I am safe and protected during this mourning rite and at all times."

Light the black candles and burn the incense. Stand or sit comfortably before the altar and say words that seem appropriate to you, according to your own spiritual tradition. (Review chapter 2 for details on grounding, centering, and casting the circle of protection.) Breathe deeply and allow your entire body to relax. Gaze at the Death card (13) and ponder what you are mourning—the reasons you are doing this rite. What is it that you grieve? What do you intend to accomplish with this ritual? When you feel relaxed and centered, say out loud: "I ask that the Dark Goddess (or Spirit of Death and Rebirth) bless and protect me during this rite. I ask for wisdom, guidance, and comfort as I deeply mourn my losses. I release the past with love and I am free. This is correct and for the good of all. May it harm none. So shall it be."

One by one, read your letters or lists aloud. Stay with the particular situation or person for a moment. When you are ready, hold up a letter or list and say something like this: "I release the past with love and I am free." Light the letter or list and place it in the fireproof dish. As it burns, feel the pain and sadness leaving you with the curls of smoke.* If you are working with a more recent wound, you can say: "I let go of this pain and I am free." Your own words are always best in ritual. Say anything that will comfort you. If you have a special prayer or spell, by all means use it. No ritual you do is sacred unless it is sacred to you.

Do not hurry this process. Stay as long as you need to. At the conclusion of this chapter, you will have an opportunity to celebrate the new present you have created, but for now, mourn your losses. Grief has its

---

* If smoke bothers you, simply tear the paper into tiny bits as you visualize and let it fall from your hands in "rain" upon the altar.

own timetable and cannot be rushed. When you are ready, thank your Spiritual Source (or Dark Goddess) for any guidance, wisdom, or comfort you may have received during the mourning rite.

Bring your attention back to the room by becoming aware of your breath. Fill your heart area with purple light and know that true healing has begun. Move your feet and place the palms of your hands on the floor to ground yourself. If you are going to be home for awhile, let the candle burn down to the socket. Dispose of the "ashes of your pain" in a ceremonious way, if you wish, but do throw them away. Change the shadow altar to white or purple to honor this rite of passage from pain to a place of healing. Place the healing energy of Temperance (14) across the Death tarot card. Put white or purple flowers there and switch to white or purple candles. Select a light and pleasant incense or one that sends out loving energy, such as rose. The shadow altar is a physical representation of your spirituality. These suggestions are only guides to help you get in touch with your inner wisdom. Use your intuition and let the shadow altar be an expression of your own healing.

Make an entry in your journal about the mourning ritual. What unexpressed emotion now has a voice? What unresolved conflict has found resolution? What shadows have you fully embraced? The next section will help you with the gifts you found in the dark.

Wish Upon a Star

In chapter 6 you embraced the shadow and discovered the light within. In this chapter, we have explored the outward expression of the inner light. What have you learned about yourself and others? With all the tools and skills you have available to you now, if you had just one wish, what would it be? This is not fantasy or wishful thinking. You have worked very hard to be where you are. Knowing what you know now, with all its clear-eyed honesty, look at your list and review what you wrote for category four: gifts that hide in the dark. With the healing energy of pure intention to guide you, what is your wish? How can the creative power of the gifts found in the dark make your wish come true? What are you now able to create? What talents and abilities have been revealed?

For centuries, gazing at the star-studded heavens has evoked secret dreams and glimpses of infinity. Once plucked from the sky, this bright symbol of creative possibility becomes your opportunity to wish upon a star. Take the Star (17) from your tarot deck. You will use it as a focus for meditation. Place it where you can see it comfortably without straining your eyes.

As always, begin by slowing your breath until you feel your entire body relax. Try this affirmation: "I open myself to my truth. Creativity is my birthright because I am one with my Spiritual Source." Look at the Star and allow the edges of the card to become blurry. Do not force this. It will happen in its own time. Enter the card, as you learned in chapter 3, and drink in the radiance of the star. Open your heart to its warmth and wisdom. Tell the star what you wish for. Listen to your voice of inner wisdom for guidance. You may be given ideas on how to make your wish come true. Stay with this beautiful star for as long as you like. After all, you have found your way to it in the dark. Enjoy the experience and let your center shine.

When you are ready, allow the lines of the card to become clear and two-dimensional again. Step back through it. Breathe deeply. Slowly become aware of the room. Move your feet and place your hands on the floor. Make an entry in your journal.

What did you wish for? What guidance did you receive about making your wish real?

In chapter 6, you looked at ways to heal yourself and discovered the light within. Chapter 7 examined a process for healing relationships and the past for outward expression of the inner light. The next (and last) chapter will explore methods to step into the world and create a bright future.

Endnotes

1. Berube, Margery S., editor. *The American Heritage Dictionary*, Second College Edition. (Boston, Houghton Mifflin Company, 1985), p. 300

Chapter 8
STAR OF HOPE

And the end of all our exploring
Will be to arrive where we started
And know the place for the first time.
T. S. Eliot

THE PURPOSE OF CHAPTER 8 IS TO EXAMINE THE POSSIBLE FUTURE WITH
a sense of realistic hope. This is not fantasy or wishful thinking. Realistic
hope is based on the healing power of pure intention and is grounded
in your Higher Self. While some events and situations cannot be
changed, the perception and meaning of those events can be changed
through the power of choice.

We begin with the final tarot layout called the Star of Hope. It will
help you plan and visualize a hopeful future. Your dreams and desires are
sacred and you have found gifts in the dark. You learn how to give physical expression to your sacred desires in a creative exercise called "The
Treasure Chest." Other activities designed to foster hope include creating a specific plan of action for the future and changing your shadow
altar. You have an opportunity to assess your growth by repeating an

exercise from chapter 3. Shadow work is an ongoing process of reclaiming the lost parts of yourself; it's never too late to exercise your power of choice.

Discovering the Creator Within

I believe we are put on earth to create—from creating a child to creating a home, a garden, a meal, an atmosphere of love, a piece of jewelry, or the life we want—it's all a divine act of creation. Shadow work is soul work and soul work is creating—and birthing—the life of "something more." Healing releases a surge of creative energy because we turn to the wisdom of our Higher Self and discover the creator within.

It can be frightening to believe we are able to construct the life we dream of by listening to our spiritual, creative, inner voice. We begin to hope, and we begin to fear that hope, because creativity carries with it the responsibility of personal choice. When we choose, we change, and it is the change that causes fear. For most of us, learning to trust the creative inner voice is the most difficult aspect of healing. The remainder of the chapter will help you to develop trust of the creator within.

The Star of Hope

The final tarot layout is designed to foster hope—not from fantasy or wishful thinking, but from a deep source of truth that springs from your Higher Self. It is hope inspired by the healing power of pure intention. You can then use the Star of Hope to plan and visualize the possible future. Allow at least twenty minutes for this exercise.

Light candles and incense to cue your unconscious that something important is about to happen. Begin by taking slow, deep breaths to achieve a state of relaxation.

Repeat the shadow work affirmation: "By embracing my shadow, I am healing and becoming whole. I am gaining wisdom and learning compassion."*

---

* By this time, you will be familiar with tarot. Commentary is limited in the final layout because it's time for the teacher to let go; trust your intuition, spread your wings, and let yourself soar to a higher overview.

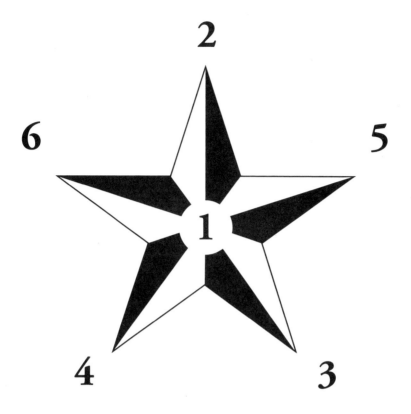

FIGURE FOUR—STAR OF HOPE

Position One—Your Hope for the Future: Place card 17, the Star, in position one; or, choose another card that speaks to you of promise and hope. Let your center shine. Shuffle the remaining twenty-one cards. As you shuffle, concentrate on making contact with the creator within. It may be helpful to chant "I create my life consciously and with love" while shuffling.

When you are ready, randomly choose five cards and place them face down in position two through six, as shown in the illustration. Be sure that the first card you draw is in position two, the second in position three, etc. Turn them over and record your initial reaction in your journal.

Position Two—Your Desire: What can I realistically be hopeful about? As with the Star of Illumination in chapter 6, you will use "the gifts that hide in the dark" in Appendix A. What is your sacred desire? What does the creator within hope to create?

Position Three—Your Gifts: What do I need to keep and nurture? What gifts have you found in the dark? What strengths have you developed? What do you love about yourself? How can you nurture and encourage the creator within?

Position Four—Your Responsibilities: What work still needs to be done? You are always a work of art in progress. What is your unfinished business? What lost part of you do you still need to recover? What part of the shadow still needs embracing? What blocks you from growth? What do you need to do to release your creator within?

Position Five—Your Potential: How will my life change as a result of embracing my shadow? What is the benefit to you in doing shadow work? What will enter your life because you have now made room for it? What wounds have healed? What lost part of you did you recover and how will this change your life? What is the forward motion of your creator within?

Position Six—Your Self-Completion: How can I shine my Star of Hope on others? How can I reach out with wisdom and compassion to other people in pain? How can I support others while allowing them their own truths? What can I create to benefit others? How can I outwardly express the divine creator within?

Make an entry in your journal. Do not try to "force" information. Breathe deeply to allow your mind to be still and receptive. Incubate a dream for more details. Leave the Star of Hope layout on your altar for awhile and record additional insights as they occur to you. Learn to listen to—and trust—your creative inner voice of healing.

The Treasure Chest

Your desire is your prayer. Picture the fulfillment of your desire now and feel its reality and you will experience the joy of the answered prayer.
Dr. Joseph Murphy

Many wonderful books have been written about creativity and planning for the life you want. Please refer to Appendix C and the bibliography for suggestions. The idea of creating an outward, physical expression of your innermost self is not a new one. This activity is designed to get you in touch with your creator within, and, if the child in you wants to come out and play during the process, so much the better.

Your dreams and desires are sacred because they arise from your most authentic self—the soul. Small rituals you do for yourself are good for the soul. When you connect to your authentic self—the creator within—you demonstrate your commitment to transforming healing energy into creative reality.

Creating your own treasure chest literally involves putting spirituality into physical form. A treasure chest will connect you to your creator within and your sacred dreams and desires. It can be as elaborate or plain as your imagination, time, money, and desire dictate. The more you do yourself, the better it will be, but if you do not want to make a treasure box yourself, go shopping for a beautiful chest. You can also use an envelope and stickers as your dream vessel. It's not the box or envelope that's magical; the magic comes from you and your pure intention of creating a healing reality.

Look back at the meditation in chapter 7 called "Wish upon a Star." What did you wish for? What is your sacred desire? What will most give expression to your creator within? What do you really want to create in your life as a result of shadow work? What can you create to let your inner light shine? Only you can know the answers.

Incubate a dream about your treasure chest or repeat the "Wish upon a Star" meditation to connect with the creator within. Look again at the Star of Hope spread at the beginning of this chapter for ideas on creating your own healing reality. Meditate with the Star of Hope spread as a focus. Listen to your inner voice of creative healing. Once you have a picture in your mind about the sacred reality you want to create, you are ready to put this spiritual expression into physical form by creating your treasure chest.

Decorate the outside of your treasure chest with pictures to symbolize your authentic self and collect items to place inside that represent your sacred desires and dreams. The treasure chest will create its own magical energy to help you manifest your desires. Keep your eyes open for things to use on or in your treasure chest. Sometimes, they will just appear in your path.

Think of the act of creating your dream vessel as a treasure hunt. Any picture, item, or object that symbolizes your goal belongs in your treasure chest. Here are a few ideas to get you started, but trust your intuition and listen to your creator within:

* Use postcards, magazines, stickers, photographs, or greeting cards for pictures that represent your dream. Photocopy images of tarot cards or draw your own.

* Browse an arts and crafts store, card shop, or toy store for inspiration.

* Start thinking in symbols: if your desire money, put a dollar bill in your treasure chest; if you want a new job, place a stone from the work site in the box; use hearts for love; toy cars for a real car; toy houses to represent your dream home; a small pocket mirror to reflect who you are; the tarot Sun card (19) if you desire health; a religious symbol for spirituality; minibooks for returning to school; incense to invoke universal forces; potpourri for a special aroma. The possibilities are endless. Trust your inner creative voice.

After you have created your treasure chest, take a pretty sheet of paper or parchment and write down your sacred desires in detail, one to a page. Light red candles and cinnamon incense for creativity, or white candles and sandalwood incense for pure intention. One at a time, place each goal in the box or envelope and invoke the healing power of pure intention by saying something like this (it is always best if you create your own poem or prayer to use in ritual):

Energy white, energy bright
Strengthening the wish I make tonight,
Its equivalent or better I ask of you.
I will do my part and follow through.
My wish is pure and made in love,
As it is below, so it is above.

Close the lid to your treasure chest and put it in a safe place where it will be undisturbed. Look at it periodically for inspiration. Revise and update your treasure chest as your goals become real, or you change your mind. (You *do* have the right to alter your plans as your future unfolds one day at a time.) The next section will suggest concrete ways to act upon your creative desires and bring them to reality.

Make an entry in your journal. Often creativity and playfulness are not valued in our hectic day-to-day existence because they take too much time, energy, and effort. If you find the treasure chest idea silly or a waste of time, be sure to explain that to yourself in detail. Make an effort to understand why you feel the way you feel.

Plan Your Plans
(and Expect the Unexpected)

You have a treasure chest to physically represent your inner most dreams. Great, now what? You are ready for the planning stage of creating a healing reality. Any inner desire you have is made real by the action you take on your own behalf. There's an old joke that goes something like this: A destitute woman prayed every day that she would win the lottery so she could feed her family and survive. She invoked spirits, recited incantations, made talismans, and generally did anything else she could think of to increase her chances of hitting the lucky number. Week after week, she didn't win and her circumstances grew more grave. Finally, in desperation, she called out to the universe, "Please, I beg the gods above to let me win the lottery, or surely my family will starve to death." All at once, the heavens opened and a big, booming voice shouted at her, "Buy a ticket!"

We can be amused by the story, but the point is, no amount of magic will make your dreams real if not accompanied by the appropriate measure of elbow grease.

My favorite writer is William Zinsser, author of *On Writing Well.* I like him because he writes so . . . well. He offers advice to writers, but one suggestion he makes is appropriate here: Never become the prisoner of a preconceived plan.[1] A popular slogan in a twelve-step group tells us to "plan plans, not results." In other words, the universe may have a better idea. When we expect the unexpected, we open ourselves up to the realm of possibilities. If we rigidly adhere to a preconceived plan, we run the risk of missing golden opportunities. We can certainly plan and have a direction, but the results may be different from anything we could ever imagine on our own.

Worry—
The Dwelling Place of Failure

I like to think of worry as being caught in the "wreckage of the future." Worry serves no useful purpose and drains us of precious time and energy that we could be using in constructive ways. Worry is the dwelling place of failure because it destroys dreams and paralyzes us with fear. Inaction is the enemy of creating a healing reality—and the life you want.

When fear raises its ugly head in the form of anxiety and worry, two things happen and they're both self-defeating, (1) your harsh inner critic tells you that changing your life is easy and you should already know how to do it; and (2) change is impossibly mystical and decided by fate, therefore you have no control over how it happens. Both outlooks paralyze us with inaction and carry a self-fulfilling prophecy of failure.

When we start our journey of change, we can be overwhelmed by unorganized thoughts, both terrifying and wonderful. To overcome being stuck in the wreckage of the future, take a close look and you dreams, goals, and desires. Write down absolutely everything you can think of that might go wrong, from not having enough money to looking silly in the eyes of your family and friends. This allows you to express worry in all its myriad forms so that you can let go of the fear and think more clearly. Once you get all your worries down on paper, you'll have the added benefit of seeing how preposterous (and unfounded) most of them really are.

Look at your list of worries. Ask yourself one question: If this is the worst thing that ever happened to me for the rest of my life, could I survive it? Given this new perspective, the answer is usually yes. Change is not an orderly and coherent process, but a complex, lovely, and sometimes frightening mess. Taking action on your own behalf, however chaotic it feels, allows expression of your sacred creator within—and that is the miracle of healing.

Planning Your Plans

In chapter 6 you explored how to think big and act small; by taking tiny steps through your power of choice, you have set in motion a powerful healing energy that feeds on your actions. The more you take small, healing steps on a daily basis, the stronger the healing force becomes. The next activity guides you in the process of thinking big and acting small.

Look at what you wrote for the Star of Illumination spread in chapter 6, the "Wish upon a Star" exercise in chapter 7, and the Star of Hope layout at the beginning of this chapter. Does it appear to be a complex, lovely, wonderful, frightening mess? Good. All creation starts in chaos.

It's time to prioritize your mess. Using the information from the three activities above, start by making a list of all your goals, in no particular order. Just write them down. Tell your harsh inner critic to be still. If it's one of your sacred desires, it belongs on the list. It may be helpful to announce out loud to the universe that you are serious by stating an affirmation of intent: "I am open to receiving love, happiness, health, and prosperity because I deserve them all. I take responsibility for my healing and create my own future."

If you are having difficulty getting started, ask yourself: What do I really want? What do I really need? Write down everything that comes to mind, big and small, from wanting a villa in the Bahamas to needing a reliable source of income.

If you're still stuck, try this visualization: it's called the "Deathbed Exercise." You are lying on a bed at your current age and you are dying. You are not in physical pain, but you are aware of the fact that in a few hours your life on earth will end. In your imagination, let your whole life pass before you. What are your accomplishments? Your failures? What did you do that gave your life real meaning? How did you waste time? What made you happy? What is the one thing you wish you had done that you did not?

Make an entry in your journal. Do you have a better picture of your sacred desires? How many of these goals are you willing to take responsibility for? How much elbow grease are you willing to apply to each one? These questions may help you to distinguish between fantasy and clear-eyed planning for the possible future.

Another technique to get you started is called brainstorming. Simply write everything down that comes to mind as you contemplate your future, however outrageous or serious. Most of us are familiar with the concept of brainstorming but few of us have any faith in it. Finish your brainstorming session by crossing out fantasy and the absurd. You may be amazed at your list. Beginning with a flow of ideas allows your creator within free expression.

Take another sheet of paper and write five time frames across the top of the page:

* Now

* Short-term (1–3 months)

* Middle ground (4–12 months)

* Long-term (1–5 years)

* Ongoing

Take all your goals and put them in their respective categories. Focus first on now and ongoing because they are the most pressing. Next concentrate on short-term goals. Think of concrete things you can do to move yourself one small step closer to your goal.

For instance, if your goal is to find a new career, you can redo your résumé and sign up for a class now. You will look for employment opportunities on an ongoing basis. In one to three months you may be taking that class. Armed with the new skills of your course, you will be at a new job in four to twelve months and your dream of self-employment is the sacred desire for one to five years from now.

You now have a map for the journey of your life. When you plan for the future, but stay in the here and now, you allow for the possibility of beautiful detours. By taking tiny steps towards the future on a daily basis, the next course of action will become apparent to you at the time you need it. Remember you have set in motion a powerful healing energy that feeds on your daily actions. Once you commit yourself to this forward motion, the universe will enthusiastically join you in the healing process.

What Have You Done for Me Lately?

We have explored worry as the dwelling place of failure, but let's examine a more sinister condition: the well-placed doubt voiced by our "loving" family and friends. It takes courage to be exceptional. We all know the doubters in our lives—the near and dear who bombard us with negative scenarios, however "well-intended" the comments may be, the "I'm only telling you this for your own good" family member, or the "Do you really believe this is practical?" friend. In *The Artist's Way* (1992), Julia Cameron writes, "Always remember: the first rule of magic is self-containment."[2]

When talking to others about your creative, healing life, ask yourself whether they are truly supportive of your efforts, or, will they cast their own shadows of doubt and envy on your path? Watch for saboteurs who try to wound you with their negative talk. Hold your intention within yourself. Talk about what you have done, not what you are going to do. Do not tolerate anyone who wants to keep you down. Share your creative healing with only your allies—and know who they are. There is power in secrecy.

Alter Your Altar

When you first created the shadow altar, you literally put spiritual expression into physical form. Is it time to change the focus of your altar? You have discovered the gifts that hide in the dark and found outward expression of the inner light. Your intuitive Higher Self is fed by images. What does the creator within want on your altar?

Your creative inner voice speaks to you in art, images, dreams, and fantasies. Altars remind you to live with purpose and to connect with your personal sense of the divine. Make the altar a sensual experience, for it is this part of you that communicates with your Spiritual Source. Everything about the altar is personal and will reflect your individuality and healing experiences. You have embraced the shadow—what will symbolize the change? Trust your intuition and let the creator within find expression.

You've Come a Long Way

Remember chapter 3? You made a journal entry called "Before You Begin."

It's purpose was to give you a compass for the first steps of your journey. Do the exercise again and compare it to the original entry. It will help you see just how far you've travelled.

Take slow deep breaths to achieve a state of relaxation. Answer these questions in your journal: Who are you? Write everything that comes to mind. Do not censor your writing. Describe your perfect self. Describe your imperfect self. What do you like about yourself? What do you dislike about yourself? What are your talents? What do you do well? Name your shadows. What is your current attitude toward the shadow? Can you see any purpose in your shadow? How has this book helped you? What have you gained from shadow work? What do you envision for your future as a result of shadow work? What do you hope for? What are the gifts that you found in the dark? Date your entry and compare it to the original one in chapter 3. How has it changed? You have embraced your shadow and the opportunities it offers. Celebrate your courage and let your inner light shine.

It's Never Too Late

> *You must be the change you wish to see in the world.*
> Mahatma Gandhi

Rose Kennedy said it best: On the occasion of her 100th birthday, she was asked to reveal her secret to longevity. To paraphrase her reply, she said: What happens to us in life is not as important as how we cope with what happens to us. Coping is everything. Coming from a woman who lost three sons to tragic death, these are wise words to ponder.

Each of us has a purpose for being here, but sometimes we fall into the trap of setting up the wrong life. This book was not written to convince anyone of anything. Instead, it asks one simple question: If you truly yearn to live the unlived life, what is stopping you? Nothing can—when you exercise your power of choice.

Endnotes

1. Zinsser, William. *On Writing Well.* Sixth Edition. (New York, HarperPerennial, 1998), p. 5

2. Cameron, Julia. *The Artist's Way.* (New York, Penguin Putnam, Inc., 1992), p. 199

Epilogue

DAWN

If the fool would persist in his folly, he would become wise.
William Blake

I BELIEVE WE ALL HAVE COMMON HUNGERS: WE LONG TO BE ACCEPTED for who we are, we ache for the healing of childhood wounds, we desire a spirituality that will put an end to our loneliness. In other words, we yearn for "something more." Shadow work is reclaiming lost parts of ourselves—images, feelings, and abilities—from the darkness of the unconscious. Instead of burying our shadow, we learn to carry our shadow through conscious choice. We are free, at last, to live the unlived life.

Congratulate yourself for having tremendous courage. Shadow work is an ongoing process of discovery, exploration, and integration. As time passes, shuffle and deal another star spread when you feel the power of the unexamined shadow working within you. Review your readings periodically.

What is the unresolved inner conflict or unexpressed emotion? How has the shadow offered you wisdom and compassion? Are you hesitant to develop your talents? What work still needs to be done? In what ways can you outwardly express the inner light? It's never too late to discover the creator within when you exercise your power of choice.

Tarot Shadow Work provides a type of "mystical therapy," a careful blending of practical advice and mysticism. Shadow work is but one method of healing. Any type of therapy or spiritual system that moves us closer to a state of wholeness is worthy of our attention. Whatever works, works.

By selecting *Tarot Shadow Work* as a companion, you have allowed me to enter your life on a deeply personal level. Thank you for that privilege. May you find peace and healing through the darkness.

PART III

STAR GUIDES

Appendix A

SHADOWS OF TAROT

Shadows of Tarot: The Challenges and Gifts

EVERY TAROT CARD HAS A SHADOW SIDE, THOUGH RARELY MENTIONED IN tarot books. The shadow is usually lumped into the Strength card (number 8 or 11, depending on your deck), the Devil (15), or the Tower (16). You also get a peek at the shadow's presence when any card appears upside-down in a conventional reading.

Tarot Shadow Work doesn't provide popular tarot definitions for cards or for their reversed meanings. Instead, we take the twenty-two cards of the major arcana (the Fool through the World) and depict the dual nature of life: by practicing light-side/dark-side thinking, we learn to hold opposites. In this reading, life is no longer a series of "yes or no," "all or nothing" questions. A gray, neutral area is born where ambiguities exist together and life starts to make sense.

Please refer to Appendix C for a recommended reading list of basic tarot texts. I've never seen one better than Mary K. Greer's *Tarot for Your Self* (1984).

All cards in a shadow reading are to be interpreted as right-side up. If a reversed (upside-down) card appears, it serves only to call attention to itself. In effect, it is saying, "Hey, look at me closely because I'm different. Examine me first. I'm the most important card in your layout." A reversed card may also mean the information is on an unconscious or psychological level, unknown to you. It may require meditation and dream work to make itself apparent. Don't be concerned if your deck has Justice as number 8 and Strength as number 11. For the purposes of shadow work, the meanings of both cards remain the same, regardless of the numbering.

Not all the listed meanings of a card will pertain to your situation. Choose one to three phrases that "ring true" and work with them first. As a rule, a tarot card will either tell you about a situation or give you advice about that situation. Consider your own insights, meanings, and images and how they might apply to your life.

FIGURE FIVE—A SAMPLE STAR SPREAD

The Fool (0)
Mistrust Versus Trust

The Fool's Shadow (challenges, when the shadow is unconscious):

* not listening to your inner voice

* fearing or doubting the future

* remaining psychologically stuck

* having a blind naïveté (immaturity or foolishness) which allows others to take advantage of you

* refusing to try the new

* lacking playfulness (being too solemn)

* rigidity

The Shadow Gifts of the Fool (opportunities to grow when the shadow is made conscious and healing energy is released):

* having an openness to divine guidance based on trust

* being willing to take a leap of faith into the unknown

* having a belief that the universe will provide you with what you need at the time you need it

* psychological growth

* having spontaneity and a sense of playfulness

* listening to your inner child

* willing to take risks and try something new without knowing the outcome because you trust the process

* abandoning old ways of thinking

Note: The phrase appearing in italic letters after the name of each card in Appendix A refers to oppositions—opposing forces created by all-or-nothing thinking. In shadow work, this yes-or-no outlook is transcended, giving the practitioner the ability to tolerate ambiguity where yes and no exist together. Result: life starts to make sense.

The Magician (1)
Lack of Focus Versus Focus

The Magician's Shadow:

* not applying your energy and efforts in the right direction

* being scattered

* lacking focus and not focusing on the real issue

* pessimism

* using trickery or deceit to accomplish goals

* indirectness

* abusing power for selfish gain

* starting many projects and not being able to complete them due to lack of motivation

* at the worst, the shadow of the Magician is dishonest about motives and can be destructive in relationships

The Shadow Gifts of the Magician:

* being able to prioritize and make a choice

* taking action on your own behalf, rather than simply wishing for change or success

* knowing there is always more to a situation than meets the eye

* being able to focus your energy effectively to accomplish your goals

* creating order out of chaos

* being able to make your own reality by using a surge of creative energy

* the ability to visualize your goals clearly

* being aware of the inner guide

* seeing your own potential and being able to visualize the work required to manifest it

* the ability to plan and carry out those plans

* working to make your goals real

* being practical, energetic, insightful, spiritual, and emotionally mature—all at the same time

* discovering the creator within

The High Priestess (2)
Superficiality Versus Intuition

The Shadow of the High Priestess:

* being too literal or intellectual

* an inability to trust intuition

* not looking below the surface

* being unwilling to explore the unconscious

* an inability to acknowledge the masculine/feminine aspect of the personality

* being vague or so caught up in your intuitive nature that you have difficulty living in the real, day-to-day world

* disliking women

* secretive behavior

* rejection of all things esoteric

* superficiality

The Shadow Gifts of the High Priestess:

* having complete faith in your intuition

* making logical decisions based on your intuition

* involvement with a group of women

* exploring the unconscious

* seeking hidden knowledge through dreams, images, feelings, art, tarot, or astrology

* seeking a counselor to help you explore things unseen

* balancing the intellect and intuition

The Empress (3)
Smothering Versus Mothering

The Shadow of the Empress:

* being a controlling, powerful woman

* the archetype of the Wicked Stepmother

* focused on others so much that self-nurturance is neglected

* smothering others with a "love" that stifles individuality
* being unable to let go of relationships
* emotional neediness
* dwelling on the pains of the past
* not allowing for the opinions of others
* feeling emotionally barren
* destroying rather than creating
* holding on to destructive situations

The Shadow Gifts of the Empress:

* the archetype of the Great Mother
* now is the time to establish yourself in relationship to others
* she is the part of you who knows how to create what you need
* a time to nourish yourself as well as others
* the creator within
* a time to heal family relationships
* fertility of mind, body, or emotions
* letting go of the need to control
* creating rather than destroying
* a time to get in touch with your body and sensuality
* nurturing individuality
* allowing others their own truths

The Emperor (4)
Rigidity Versus Stability

The Shadow of the Emperor:

* being disenchanted with life

* out of touch with feelings, lacking a sense of wonder or adventure

* intellect without imagination

* controlling others aggressively
* depending on others to control your behavior
* difficulty making decisions
* confusing authority with domination
* becoming angry when someone disagrees with you or challenges your authority
* exercising extreme self-control or none at all
* controlling father figure
* unreceptive to others
* stubbornness

The Shadow Gifts of the Emperor:

* placing mind over matter
* being a respected authority figure
* building something real and solid
* energetic, imaginative, and assertive
* having the life force to strive and succeed
* having a clear-eyed view of reality
* giving form and structure to your life
* having a concrete idea or plan, with well-deserved power
* being outwardly directed
* accepting responsibility for your actions
* using logic to solve problems
* loving father figure
* leadership abilities, especially at work

The Hierophant (5)
Fanaticism Versus Inner Conscience

The Shadow of the Hierophant:

* intolerance toward people whose religious viewpoint differs from yours

* being a "groupie," that is, placing too much emphasis on affiliations, and getting stuck in the rhetoric of a group

* adopting principles without thinking them through or considering what they really mean in your life

* blindly following rules without thinking through the consequences

* being overly concerned with outer appearances

* exhibiting hostility toward the established order while lacking an inner guide

* going against your true beliefs in order to gain acceptance of a group

* blind faith and dogmatism

* spiritual corruption, while repressing the spiritual values of yourself or others

* casting off the religion or traditions of your childhood without first examining them for insight

* being without conscience or principles

The Shadow Gifts of the Hierophant:

* having an inner conscience that guides you and finding meaning within the established order

* searching for a spiritual or personal philosophy that is accessible through word, book, lecture, or service

* having a carefully thought out and studied personal philosophy that guides you rather than rules you

* conforming to a belief system or group because your Higher Self dictates it

* informed participation in a group rather than blind obedience

* finding value in the religion or traditions of your childhood because you have questioned and thoroughly examined them

* asking your inner teacher for guidance

The Lovers (6)
Disharmony Versus Responsible Choices

The Shadow of the Lovers:

* being unable to make a choice, to trust love, or to risk losing control

* feeling cut off from guidance because you are using only the conscious intellect

* choosing irresponsibly

* refusing to look at life's opposites or feeling out of balance

* cutting yourself off from emotions which can lead to depression

* infidelity

* inability to get close in a relationship, and domination or power plays in relationships

* difficulty recognizing conflicting aspects of yourself or not loving yourself

* disharmony produced by indecision or poor choices

* resistance to any type of therapy which might produce integration of conflicting forces

The Shadow Gifts of the Lovers:

* understanding that both the intellect and intuition are important for guidance

* making responsible choices, especially in relationships

* being able to identify the opposites needed for balance in any situation

* becoming aware of the loving nature of your Higher Self

* the choice of loving yourself, and being able to risk loving

* making a responsible decision about a love relationship

* the marriage of mind and spirit

* looking to your Higher Self for guidance

* the coming together of opposite qualities that leads to wholeness

* the ability to negotiate

* trusting love

* having a relationship based on equality

* the moving of your consciousness from your intellect to your heart

The Chariot (7)
Conflict Versus Balanced Control

The Chariot's Shadow:

* not understanding or controlling the opposites within you

* inflated ego

* prohibitive hubris

* a self-control based in denial

* strength and authority that come from "out there" somewhere and not within

* conflict within and conflict with others

* struggles and battles that seem to have no purpose

* lack of self-control

* not having a sense of direction in your life

* wanting to control others

* unwillingness to consider another view

* charging ahead without doing your research

* inappropriate aggression or force

* making demands without self-reflection

The Shadow Gifts of the Chariot:

* solving a present problem using the skills of your past experiences

* considering a problem from someone else's viewpoint

* activism

* triumph and victory through hard work

* groundedness based on an inner knowing

* ying/yang: knowing the necessity of positive and negative forces (opposites) to balance life and cause growth within

* strength and independence based on taking a full look at yourself

* learning about yourself (inner work) through the involvement with others (outer work)

* strength and authority coming from within

Strength (8 or 11)
Rage Versus Compassion

Strength's Shadow:

* lack of courage or integrity

* insecurity

* destructive aggression

* rage, possibly expressed in abusiveness or sexual abuse

* lack of compassion or selfishness

* violent tendencies and hate

* relying too much on instincts

* being afraid of your instinctual (or animal) nature

* denying the existence of a lower self

* denying the existence of the unconscious

* becoming a victim of your untamed nature by fearing it

The Shadow Gifts of Strength:

* finding a way to make your animal nature a peaceful companion

* making peace with the dark side of your nature and extending that compassion to others

* the power to help others by first helping yourself

* being compassionate with yourself when you make mistakes

* being compassionate with others for making mistakes

* having courage, strength, and self-discipline

* potential for mastery of a problem

* self-awareness

* learning how to make contact with the unconscious

* making something tangible out of something heard inside

* being grounded and centered

* psychic centers are about to open

* having dignity

* leadership abilities based on compassion

* having an inner strength that allows you to heal yourself and others

The Hermit (9)
Fear of the Dark Versus Patient Solitude

The Hermit's Shadow:

* fear of isolation and boredom

* fear of being alone with your thoughts and feelings

* fear of introspection

* spiritual emptiness

* engaging in meaningless activity or trying to make the meaning-less more important than it is

* extreme dependence on a spiritual leader or guru

* extreme dependence on a psychic counselor, tarot reader, or astrologer

* overinflated pride for having religious experiences

* cutting yourself off from the world because you don't like people

* running away from your problems

* being unable to evaluate a situation because you don't have clear goals

* unable to accept aging or death

* impatience, depression, indecision

The Shadow Gifts of the Hermit:

* seeking solitude to find inner strength

* accepting the natural rhythm of life, including aging and death

* being at a crossroads of decision and renewal

* the ability to solve your own problems by introspection and lis-tening to your own guidance

* in withdrawing, you prepare for a way out of the dark

* finding an individual light when established religions fail you

* a spiritual climb that makes you a lantern in the dark for others

* radiating a higher force

* finding a spiritual leader or guru

* seeking the advice of a psychic, tarot reader, or astrologer

* having inner wisdom

* accepting solitude as freeing rather than fear of the dark

* using meditation as a way to understanding

The Wheel of Fortune (10)
Blame Versus Change

The Shadow of the Wheel of Fortune:

* believing yourself to be a victim of fate

* feeling stuck in a rut

* fighting change

* lacking the persistence necessary to carry out tasks

* unable to roll with the punches of life

* not recognizing opportunities

* unable to finish what you start

* not cleaning up loose ends, especially with relationships

* getting caught in the trivia of life

* unable to accept change as a natural cycle of life

* wishing everything would stay the same

* blaming others or "fate" for what befalls you

* missing the big picture

* holding on to the past

The Shadow Gifts of the Wheel of Fortune:

* understanding that there is an orderly plan behind the seemingly random changes of your life

* accepting the cyclical nature of time and change: every situation has the potential for learning

* knowing you are a part of an ever-changing process

* accepting responsibility for what befalls you without blaming fate

* realizing that the more you know about your inner self, the more you choose your own destiny

* observing the overall pattern of your life instead of the details

* a fortunate new beginning

* a new chapter in your life is starting

* understanding cause and effect and directing your life accordingly

Justice (11 or 8)
Imbalance Versus Balance

The Shadow of Justice:

* being overly concerned with the "fairness" of your situation

* an inability to accept the consequences of your actions

* leaping to a hasty decision without weighing all the factors

* lack of balance in your life

* not taking into account extenuating circumstances

* being so concerned with fairness that you shut out compassion and mercy

* needing a balanced mind

* lacking conscience

* using only cold logic to make a decision, or being illogical

* not being able to weigh and balance difficult decisions

* being out of touch with your Higher Self

* unclear thinking processes or prejudice

* all-or-nothing viewpoint

* going to one extreme or the other

The Shadow Gifts of Justice:

* having the ability to be make adjustments in your life

* a balanced intellect

* having clarity of mind and the ability to make fair decisions

* being reasonable

* weighing and balancing difficult decisions

* impartiality

* setting things right

* making amends

* blending your Higher Self with daily thinking to produce harmony

* being a mediator

* being true to yourself

The Hanged Man (12)
Pride Versus Humility

The Hanged Man's Shadow:

* being plunged into a state of despair when things don't go your way

* being "hung up" by circumstances where old behaviors are no longer working

* allowing pride to get in the way of personal growth

* an inability to consider change

* rigidly holding on to old values

* an unwillingness to make the necessary sacrifices or do the work necessary for success

* sacrificing too much of yourself

* futile struggling over a situation over which you actually have no control

* placing more importance on the exterior life than the interior one

The Shadow Gifts of the Hanged Man:

* being able to look at something from another angle

* considering another viewpoint

* understanding that success requires a sacrifice

* being willing to make a sacrifice for a larger goal

* deliberate turning toward the Higher Self and asking for help

* losing pride to gain humility

* making a conscious choice which will have far-reaching consequences

* allowing things to happen without the need to control

* coming to grips with unconscious forces within you

* being suspended in time and being able to tolerate that suspension

* sacrificing comfort for a greater good

Death (13)
Stagnation Versus Transformation

The Shadow of Death:

* blocking out sad feelings

* staying stuck

* fear of losing the old

* an unwillingness to move on

* fearing change and allowing that fear to control you

* not being able to let go of what is no longer useful

* living in the past

* physical or mental stagnation

* inertia

* mourning too long as a way to avoid moving forward

* the mask you wear and show to the world

* an unwillingness to experience emotional pain

* losing opportunities because of an unwillingness to change

The Shadow Gifts of Death:

* letting go of the old to make way for the new

* saying goodbye and relinquishing in love

* tuning in to the process of rebirth

* allowing yourself to mourn

* understanding that nothing ever dies, it only transforms

* being comforted during a sad time with valid insights

* realizing it is the end of a relationship, situation, or way of thinking/feeling, and new beginnings will follow the grieving period

* unfolding the mystery of transition—between the old and the new lies mourning

* recognizing it's time to let go of outdated habits, actions, and attitudes

* being open to change and the opportunities it brings

Temperance (14)
Overindulgence Versus Easy Does It

The Shadow of Temperance:

*   having a tendency to feel powerful when everything is going your way

*   not allowing emotions to flow, so they get stuck in depression or erupt in violence

* denying a dialogue between yourself and your higher consciousness

* giving undue weight to one emotion

* being uncooperative

* taking action without thought to the consequences

* having mood swings

* overindulgence and addictions

* having no patience

* being self-centered

* feeling out of control

* conflict and struggle in relationships

The Shadow Gifts of Temperance:

* using moderation and self-restraint

* striving for emotional balance

* not rushing or overdoing

* allowing higher consciousness to flow freely into conscious thought

* performing service for others without thought of selfish gains

* living a spiritual life, but being concerned with human matters, too

* learning how to balance life's opposites

* deciding to do something because you want to test yourself

* having harmony within relationships

* taking a moderate approach—easy does it, but do it

* allowing the healing process to unfold in its own time

The Devil (15)

Fear and Separation Versus Love and Connectedness

The Devil's Shadow:

* being chained to your fear, thoughts, and feelings

* failure to love yourself

* being chained to material goods

* being in bondage to negative thought patterns, habits, situations, or relationships

* having an issue with power—controlling or being controlled

* allowing yourself to be victimized

* being too serious about life

* the inability to play

* cutting yourself off from others by greed or ambition

* having ambition turn to greed or the need for power

* being the aggressor

* repressed sexuality

The Shadow Gifts of the Devil:

* removing the blocks of fear and separateness, causing great growth

* understanding your own light side/dark side which leads to compassion for others

* confronting your own negative reality and breaking free of the bondage

* accepting your need to lighten up and play

* having a choice to do things differently

* finding the discipline and courage to break free of negative habits and stuck ways of thinking

* having a confrontation with the inner world

* learning to love yourself and others

* expressing your sexuality with joy

* exercising free will to foster growth

* feeling connected to other people and less to material goods

The Tower (16)
Destruction Versus Liberation

The Tower's Shadow:

* having false philosophies or old goals which prevent you from seizing new opportunities

* building a fortress of false security around you

* lacking insight

* destroying the possibility of new growth by rigidly holding on to ideas or attitudes

* avoidance of change

* presenting a false image of yourself to others

* falling apart or breaking down when things change

* releasing repressed energy in an angry or destructive way

* seeking permanence in impermanent things

* being conventional to the point of being rigid

The Shadow Gifts of the Tower:

* breaking down unhealthy beliefs to liberate your true self

* having a flash of illumination

* breaking through old ways of thinking

* changing false structures and finding true values

* exercising free choice

* living your own chosen way rather than by convention

* releasing repressed energy that is exciting and dynamic

* seeing things in a new light

* making room for the unexpected

* presenting your true self to others

* soul-searching

* finding inner strength and spiritual meaning in tragedy and loss

* realizing nothing is permanent except the spirit

* seeking divine truth

* having sudden insight

The Star (17)
Denial and Despair Versus Healing and Hope

The Star's Shadow:

* denying the reality of a situation or issue

* failing to recognize your talents and abilities

* feelings of despair

* loss of hope

* loss of self-esteem

* getting lost in wishful thinking, fantasy, or idealism

* pessimism and lacking faith

* seeing life as pointless

* failure to open to both inner and outer truths

* failing to align with higher consciousness

* lack of self-confidence

The Shadow Gifts of the Star:

* an opportunity for new insight into a situation

* reliance on your higher consciousness for renewal

* participation in your own healing

* gaining a sense of direction

* having a renewed sense of hope based on an inner focus and outer awareness

* inspiration

* belief in a new and better life

* keeping a sense of equilibrium when life is at a low ebb

* having a sense of purpose

* feeling connected to your Spiritual Source

* the calm after the storm

* removing all fear

* having compassion

* discovering the inner light and the healing heart

The Moon (18)
Confusion Versus Mystery

The Shadow of the Moon:

* time of doubt and confusion about your feelings

* wondering if you are having spiritual experiences or are going crazy

* the unconscious in its uncontrolled aspects

* a feeling of madness

* an uncomfortable fluctuation between feelings

* indecision and passivity

* failure to acknowledge sensitivity or imagination

* resistance to recognizing the shadow

* mood swings, depression, or lunacy

* difficulty accepting the esoteric meaning of some experiences or feelings

* feeling as though everything is clouded or vague

* avoidance of intense feelings

* not acknowledging the cycles of your life

* unreceptive to information from dreams

* being vulnerable to the advice from others, even if it's not in your best interest

The Shadow Gifts of the Moon:

* the moon's essence is reflection; cold, but by her light we see our shadows

* realizing solutions may be intuitive rather than logical

* being open to information from dreams

* trusting feelings and intuition

* being open to the mysteries of your life

* failing intellect when facing the darkness and realization that only intuitive insight can uncover the depths

* relying on intuition for guidance

* recognizing the changes and cycles of your life

* having vivid memories that help you understand your situation

The Sun (19)
Burnout Versus Golden Understanding

The Shadow of the Sun:

* burnout—feeling as though you are just surviving rather than thriving

* feeling overcome with the responsibilities of your life

* lacking creativity

* burning your candle at both ends (expending your energy with such intensity that you eventually burn out)

* failing to listen to your inner child

* feeling no joy in life

* rejecting the idea that your are connected to the universe and the people in it

* not wanting to try different experiences

* being attached to the little hurts of life

* seeing the world as an obstacle to overcome

* keeping secrets that eventually burn you

* overcoming people with your energy and personality

The Shadow Gifts of the Sun:

* optimism, positive energy, and action

* to become a child again and see the world with joy, not as an obstacle to overcome

* raising the consciousness of golden understanding; calm self-confidence and personal power because you understand your place in the universe

* being able to impart form and structure out of a chaotic mess

* reconnecting with your Higher Self which yields a direct experience with your Spiritual Source

* being successful

* revealing your true self to others

* having no need for secrecy

* feeling as though life has opened up because of some positive action that you took in your own behalf

* having abundant energy

Judgement (20)
Paying the Piper Versus Rebirth

Judgement's Shadow:

* having a harsh inner critic

* focusing on what is being lost in any situation

* failing to be merciful or forgiving with yourself or others

* being too hard on yourself

* seeking revenge or divine retribution on someone who has hurt you

* staying stuck in hate

* being mired in a personal point of view that you refuse to give up

* projecting the shadow on others and judging them harshly

* being critical of others

* an unwillingness to see your own shortcomings

* refusing to apologize

* holding a grudge

* having value judgments that keep you stuck in the same place

* feeling isolated from your Spiritual Source

* seeking to punish yourself or others, as in paying the piper

The Shadow Gifts of Judgement:

* making amends

* clearing the slate of past actions

* paying debts that need to be paid

* reaching conclusions, summing up, hindsight

* a spiritual rebirth and renewal based on taking responsibility for your actions and choices

* an honest and sincere self-appraisal

* reaping what you have sewn

* focusing on what is being gained, rather than what is being lost, in any situation

* an increased awareness that leads to increased responsibility and more choices

The World (21)
Chasing a Rainbow Versus
The Challenge of Living Here

The World's Shadow:

* life is what happens to you as you are busy making other plans

* missing the joy of the moment

* looking for happiness outside yourself

* wishful thinking

* chasing impossible rainbows

* clinging to earthly security

* forgetting what it took to get you this far

* repressing painful memories

* seeking a perfection that is not attainable

* hanging on to the past

* feeling overwhelmed by the problems of the world

* the inability to recognize all aspects of yourself

* fear of restriction

* emotional stagnation and resting on your laurels

* not taking charge of your life and choices

* staying attached to people or ideas that hurt you

* being caught up in your own tiny world unable to see the big picture

The Shadow Gifts of the World:

* feeling untouched by human problems, yet fully capable of dealing with them

* wearing the world like a loose garment

* a feeling that nothing can overwhelm you now

* the completion of one cycle and the beginning of another

* standing on solid ground inside yourself

* being a whole person—not perfect, but complete

* realizing your goals

* without attachment, you are able to let go of the past and dance into the future but equilibrium at its center

Appendix B
YOU ARE
NOT ALONE

Resources and Support for Life's Tough Questions

WOUNDS FROM THE PAST CAN CAUSE OVERWHELMING PAIN. ASKING FOR help when you need it is an act of courage and sign of strength. Whatever works, works. If you need help for life's tough questions, get it. Don't hold yourself back from being all you can be.

This directory is for information and education. Except for a few "hotlines," these numbers and addresses are not meant to be used in times of acute crisis. If you feel like physically hurting yourself or harming another, this is a true psychiatric emergency. You need to go immediately to the nearest emergency room for help.

The resources listed here cover a variety of issues that may surface during shadow work. It is divided into three categories, (1) names and addresses of national support and educational organizations; (2) toll-free "hotline" phone numbers; and (3) on-line information sources. (*Note:* the internet is constantly changing; all websites were accurate at the time this book went to press.)

This is not meant to be an all-inclusive list. Wounds come in a variety of shapes and sizes. If your issue or concern isn't here, check your local Yellow Pages for services in your area or search the web for more information.

Organizations

Alcoholism

Al-Anon Family Group Headquarters
1600 Corporate Landing Parkway
Virginia Beach, VA 23454-5617
(800) 344-2666
World Directory Meeting Line: (800) 356-9996

* Lots of free information for friends and families of alcoholics. Referral to a twelve-step self-help support meeting in your area.

Alcoholics Anonymous (AA), Worldwide Services
475 Riverside Drive
New York, NY 10115
(212) 870-3400
Internet: http://www.alcoholicsanonymous.org

* AA is a twelve-step, self-help support group for alcoholics. Free information plus referral to a meeting in your area.

Alternative Medicine

Office of Alternative Medicine Clearinghouse,
National Institutes of Health
P.O. Box 8218
Silver Spring, MD 20907-8218
(888) 644-6226
Fax-back service: (301) 402-2466

* The OAM has free information and a newsletter. The fax-back service will send you the details.

Death and Loss

Association for Death Education and Counseling
638 Prospect Avenue
Hartford, CT 06105-7503
(860) 586-7503
Fax: (860) 586-7550
E-mail: ADECoffice@aol.com

* This is a professional organization in bereavement and they can refer you to a certified grief counselor. They also have information about grief.

Domestic Violence

National Coalition Against Domestic Violence
P.O. Box 18749
Denver, CO 80218-0749
(303) 839-1852

* Publishes a national directory of domestic violence programs and will put you in touch with a program in your area. They are active in public policy.

Eating Disorders

Eating Disorder Awareness and Prevention
603 Stewart Street
Seattle, WA 98101
(206) 382-3587

* This nonprofit organization offers free information and is focused on education and awareness.

Mental Health

American Psychological Association
750 First Street, NE
Washington, DC 20002-4242
(800) 374-2721
Internet: The APA Help Center at http:// www.helping.apa.org

* Will refer you to a psychologist in your area. Send a SASE (business-sized envelope) to Public Communications at the above address and they will mail you a pamphlet called "Finding Help: How to Choose a Psychologist," or you can download it at their website.

National Mental Health Association
1021 Prince Street
Alexandria, VA 22314-2971
(800) 969-6642
Internet: http://www.nmha.org

* A nonprofit advocacy organization that provides information on mental health issues and nationwide referrals.

Hotlines
(All numbers are toll-free unless otherwise stated)

Child Find

(800) 426-5678

National Child Abuse Hotline

(800) 4-A-CHILD (422-4453)

National Domestic Violence Hotline

(800) 799-SAFE (799-7233)

National Drug and Alcohol Treatment Hotline

(800) 662-HELP (662-4357)

National Health Information Center Hotline

(800) 336-4797
(has 100 health hotlines)

National Runaway Switchboard

(800) 621-4000

Nightline

(800) 273-AIDS (273-2437)
(HIV/AIDS suicide prevention)

Project Inform HIV/AIDS Treatment Hotline

(800) 822-7422

RAINN

(800) 656-HOPE (656-4673)
(Rape, Abuse, Incest and Neglect Network)

Websites

(Please see Organizations for more listings)

Medscape:

http://www.medscape.com

* A site devoted to traditional medicine and research, Medscape produces a booklet called "The HIV/AIDS Resources National Directory." Click HIV/AIDS, then Patient Resources. You must register, but Medscape is free to join and free to use.

Health A to Z :

http://www.healthatoz.com

* A comprehensive health site—everything from Alzheimer's to zinc dosages. Has both traditional and nontraditional information (listed under "Alternative Medicine"). Easy to use—just click and go. Many links. For nonmedical people and the "cyberspace-challenged" among us. Open your health search here.

For Women

WWWomen:

http://www.wwwomen.com

* This is a huge search directory for women that covers everything from diversity and sexual preferences to health and spirituality. You name it, you can find it here with a keyword search.

Appendix C
RECOMMENDED READING

Departures

I HOPE *TAROT SHADOW WORK* HAS PIQUED YOUR INTEREST AND AROUSED your curiosity about other subjects. Books appearing here are not included in the footnotes or bibliography. Don't be limited by these suggestions; instead, allow the topics to start a chain reaction of glorious exploration. Treat yourself to a library or bookstore visit, use the reading list as your launching point and see where it will lead you. Happy journey!

Creating the Life You Want

Choquette, Sonia. *Your Heart's Desire.* Three Rivers Press, 1997.

Lloyd, Carol. *Creating a Life Worth Living.* Harper Perennial, 1997.

Creative Visualization/Guided Imagery

Denning and Phillips. *Llewellyn's Practical Guide to Creative Visualization: For the Fulfillment of Your Desires.* Llewellyn Publications, 1980.

Gawain, Shakti. *Creative Visualization: Use the Power of Your Imagination to Create What You Want in Life.* Bantam Books, 1982.

Dreams and Dream Work

Delaney, Gayle, Ph.D. *All About Dreams: Everything You Need to Know About Why We Have Them, What They Mean and How to Get Them to Work for You.* HarperSanFrancisco, 1998.

Guiley, Rosemary Ellen. *Dreamwork for the Soul: A Spiritual Guide to Dream Interpretation.* Berkeley Publishers, 1998.

Earth Religions

Adler, Margot. *Drawing Down the Moon.* Beacon Press, 1986

Cunningham, Scott. *Wicca: A Guide for the Solitary Practitioner.* Llewellyn Publications, 1988.

Starhawk. *The Spiral Dance: A Rebirth of the Ancient Religion of the Great Goddess.* HarperSanFrancisco, 1989.

Eastern Religions

Boucher, Sandy. *Opening the Lotus: A Woman's Guide to Buddhism.* Beacon Press, 1997.

Forgiveness

Borysenko, Joan, Ph.D. *Seventy Times Seven: On the Spiritual Art of Forgiveness.* Sounds True, 1996. (Audio cassette: can be ordered through your local bookstore.)

For Men

Barzan, Robert, Editor. *Sex and Spirit: Exploring Gay Men's Spirituality.* White Crane, 1995.

Hollis, James. *Under Saturn's Shadow: The Wounding and Healing of Men.* Book World, 1994.

Liebman, Wayne. *Tending the Fire: The Ritual Men's Group.* Alley Press, 1991.

Tracy, David. *Remaking Men: Jung Spirituality and Social Change.* Routledge, 1997.

For Women

Cames, Robin. *Sacred Circles: A Guide to Creating Your Own Women's Spirituality Group.* HarperSanFrancisco, 1998.

Kidd, Sue Monk. *The Dance of the Dissident Daughter: A Woman's Journey from Christian Tradition to the Sacred Feminine.* HarperSanFrancisco, 1996.

Stein, Diane. *The Woman's Spirituality Handbook.* Llewellyn Publications, 1986.

Woodman, Marion, with Jill Mellick. *Coming Home to Myself: A Reflection for Nurturing a Woman's Body and Soul.* Conari Press, 1998.

Healing

Brennan, Barbara Ann. *Light Emerging: The Journey of Personal Healing*. Bantam Books, 1993.

Schultz, Mona Lisa. *Awakening Intuition: Using Your Mind-Body Network For Health and Insight*. Crown Publishers, 1998.

Stein, Diane. *All Women are Healers: A Comprehensive Guide to Natural Healing*. Crossing Press, 1990.

Journaling

Booth, Patsy R. *Tapestry: Directed Journaling for Life Weavers*. Cedar Tree Publishing, 1994.

Finlayson, Judith. *The New Woman's Diary: A Journal for Women in Search of Themselves*. Crown Publishing Group, 1994.

Jungian Psychology

(includes shadow and archetypes—please see Bibliography)

Fordham, Frieds. *An Introduction to Jungian Psychology*. Vicking Pen, 1976.

Robertson, Robin. *Your Shadow*. ARE Press, 1997.

Loss and Grief

(start with *any* book by Elisabeth Kubler-Ross, M.D.)

Harris, Eleanor L. *Pet Loss: A Spiritual Guide*. Llewellyn Publications, 1997.

Kennedy, Alexandra. *Losing A Parent: Passage to a New Way of Living*. HarperSanFrancisco, 1991.

Kluger-Bell, Kim. *Unspeakable Losses: Understanding the Experience of Pregnancy Loss, Miscarriage and Abortion.* W.W. Norton and Company, 1998.

Kowalski, Gary. *Goodbye, Friend: Healing Wisdom for Anyone Who Has Ever Lost a Pet.* Stillpoint Publishing, 1997.

Starhawk, et al. *The Pagan Book of Living and Dying: Practical Rituals, Prayers, Blessings and Meditations on Crossing Over.* HarperSanFrancisco, 1997.

Meditation

Gawain, Shatki. *Meditations: Creative Visualization and Meditations to Enrich Your Life.* New World Library, 1990.

Merrill Redfield, Salle. *The Joy of Meditating: A Beginner's Guide to the Art of Meditation.* Warner Books, Inc., 1995.

Sacred Art

Kaff-Chaplin, Deborah. *Drawing Out Your Soul: The Touch Drawing Handbook.* The Center for Touch Drawing, 1996.

Sacred Space

Linn, Denise. *Sacred Space: Clearing and Enhancing the Energy of Your Home.* Ballantine Books, Inc., 1995.

Tarot

(start with *Tarot for Your Self* by Mary K. Greer—please refer to Bibliography)

Fairfield, Gail. *Choice Centered Tarot.* Samuel Weiser, Inc., 1997.

Greer, Mary K. *Tarot Constellations: Patterns of Personal Destiny.* Newcastle Publishing, 1987.

———. *Tarot Mirrors: Reflections of Personal Meaning.* Newcastle Publishing, 1988.

Nichols, Sally. *Jung and Tarot.* Samuel Weiser, Inc., 1980.

Sharman-Burke, Juliet. *The Complete Book of Tarot.* St. Martin's Press, 1985.

Tarot Organizations

American Tarot Association
P.O. Box 17164
Boulder, CO 80308-0164
(303) 938-1408

International Tarot Society
P.O. Box 1475
Morton Grove, IL 60053
(847) 965-9916

Send either organization a SASE for membership details.

Other Resources

Mary Katherine Greer
Tools and Rites of Transformation (T.A.R.O.T.)
T.A.R.O.T. Newsletter
P.O. Box 720
Nevada City, CA 95959
Website: **http://www.nccn.net/~tarot**

> Newsletter with reviews, calendar of events, and anything else concerning tarot and women's mysteries. Send $4 for sample copy and subscription information.
>
> Tarot news, reviews, resources, spreads, events, workshops, how-to's, decks (including a beautiful one designed by her partner, Ed Buryn), an interpretation clinic and publications of Mary K. Greer. (Information provided by permission of Ms. Greer.)

BIBLIOGRAPHY

Ackroyd, Eric. *A Dictionary of Dream Symbols*. London: Wellington House (distributed in the U.S. by Sterling Publishing Company), 1993.

Angeles, Arrien. *The Tarot Handbook*. New York: Penguin Putnam, Inc., 1997.

Angelo, Jack. *Hands-On Healing: A Practical Guide to Channeling Your Healing Energies*. Rochester, Vermont: Healing Arts Press, 1997.

Berube, Margery S., editor. *The American Heritage Dictionary*. Second College Edition. Boston: Houghton Mifflin Company, 1985.

Bulfinch, Thomas and Edmund Fuller, editor. *Bulfinch's Mythology: A Modern Abridgment.* New York: Dell Publishing Company, Inc., 1963.

Cabot, Laurie. *Celebrate the Earth.* New York: Dell Publishing, 1994.

————. *Love Magic: The Way to Love through Rituals, Spells and the Magical Life.* New York: Dell Publishing, 1992.

Campbell, Eileen and J. H. Brennan. *Body, Mind and Spirit: A Dictionary of New Age Ideas, People, Places and Terms.* Boston: Charles E. Turtle Co., 1994.

Campbell, Joseph. *The Power of Myth with Bill Moyers.* New York: Doubleday, 1988.

Choquette, Sonia. *The Psychic Pathway: A Workbook for Reawakening the Voice of Your Soul.* New York: Crown Publishing Group, 1994.

Cunningham, Scott. *Cunningham's Encyclopedia of Magical Herbs.* St. Paul: Llewellyn Publications, 2000.

Echols, Signe, Robert Mueller, and Sandra Thomson. *Spiritual Tarot: Seventy-Eight Paths to Personal Development.* New York: Avon Books, 1996.

Giles, Cynthia. *The Tarot: History, Mystery and Lore.* New York: Simon and Schuster, 1992.

————. *The Tarot: Methods, Mastery and More.* New York: Simon and Schuster, 1996

Gosaferd, Michael and Brian Williams. *Light and Shadow Tarot.* Rochester, Vermont: Inner Traditions International, 1997.

Greer, Mary K. *Tarot for Your Self.* North Hollywood, California: Newcastle Publishing Company, Inc., 1984.

————. *Tarot Constellations: Patterns of Personal Destiny.* North Hollywood, California: Newcastle Publishing Company, Inc., 1987.

Gwain, Rose. *Discovering Your Self Through Tarot.* Rochester, Vermont: Destiny Books, 1994.

Hall, Calvin S. and Vernon J. Nordby. *A Primer of Jungian Psychology.* New York: Signet Mentor Books, 1973.

Hall, Judy. *The Wise Woman: A Natural Approach to the Menopause.* Rockport, Massachusetts: Element, Inc., 1992.

Harding, Ester M., M.D. *The I and Not I: A Study in the Development of the Consciousness.* New Jersey: Princeton University Press, 1965.

Hover-Kramer, Dorthea, Ed.D., RN *Healing Touch: A Resource for Health Care Professionals.* Albany, New York: Delmar Publishers, 1996.

Hunt, Morton. *The Story of Psychology.* New York: Anchor Books, Doubleday, 1994.

Joy, Brugh. *Joy's Way.* New York: G.P. Putnam's Sons, 1979.

Jung, Carl. *Collected Works.* Vols. 1–20. (R. F. C. Hull, translator) Princeton, New Jersey: Princeton University Press, Bollingen Series XX, 1953–1990.

Kaplan, Harold I., M.D. and Benjamin S. Sadock, M.D. *Synopsis of Psychiatry.* 6th Edition. Philadelphia: Williams and Wilkins, 1991.

Keegan, Lynn, Ph.D., RN *The Nurse As Healer.* Albany, New York: Delmar Publishers, 1994.

Krieger, Dolores. *The Therapeutic Touch: How to Use Your Hands to Help or to Heal.* New York: Prentice Hall Fireside Books, 1979.

Lucks, Naomi and Melene Smith. *A Woman's Midlife Companion.* Rocklin, California: Prima Publishing, 1997.

MacKinnon, Roger A., M.D. and Robert Michels, M.D. *The Psychiatric Interview in Clinical Practice.* Philadelphia: W.B. Saunders Company, 1971.

Mazza, Joan. *Dreaming Your Real Self: A Personal Approach to Dream Interpretation.* New York: Penguin Putnam, Inc., 1998.

Nichols, Sally. *Jung and Tarot: An Archetypal Journey.* York Beach, Maine: Samuel Weiser, Inc., 1980.

Noble, Vicki. *Making Ritual with Motherpeace Cards.* New York: Three Rivers Press, Random House, 1998.

Pascal, Eugene. *Jung to Live By: A Guide to the Practical Application of Jungian Principles for Everyday Life.* New York: Warner Books, 1992.

Pollack, Rachel. *Seventy-Eight Degrees of Wisdom: A Book of Tarot.* San Francisco: Thorsons HarperCollins, 1983.

Reber, Arthur S. *Dictionary of Psychology.* New York: Penguin Books, 1985.

Roach, Sally and Beatriz Nicto. *Healing and the Grief Process.* Albany, New York: Delmar Publishers, 1997.

Roderick, Timothy. *Dark Moon Mysteries: Wisdom, Power and Magic of the Shadow World.* St. Paul: Llewellyn Publications, 1996.

Stein, Diane. *The Women's Book of Healing.* St. Paul: Llewellyn Publications, 1994.

Streep, Peg. *Altars Made Easy.* San Francisco: HarperCollins, 1997.

Zinsser, William. *On Writing Well.* Sixth Edition. New York: HarperCollins, 1998.

Zweig, Connie and Jeremiah Abrams, editors. *Meeting the Shadow: The Hidden Power of the Dark Side of Human Nature.* New York: Penguin Putnam Books, 1996.

Zweig, Connie and Steve Wolf. *Romancing the Shadow: Illuminating the Dark Side of the Soul.* New York: Ballantine Books, 1997.

INDEX

217

☽ REACH FOR THE MOON

Llewellyn publishes hundreds of books on your favorite subjects! To get these exciting books, including the ones on the following pages, check your local bookstore or order them directly from Llewellyn.

ORDER BY PHONE
- Call toll-free within the U.S. and Canada, 1-800-THE MOON
- In Minnesota, call (651) 291-1970
- We accept VISA, MasterCard, and American Express

ORDER BY MAIL
- Send the full price of your order (MN residents add 7% sales tax) in U.S. funds, plus postage & handling to:

  Llewellyn Worldwide
  P.O. Box 64383, Dept. K408-1
  St. Paul, MN 55164–0383, U.S.A.

POSTAGE & HANDLING
(For the U.S., Canada, and Mexico)
- $4.00 for orders $15.00 and under
- $5.00 for orders over $15.00
- No charge for orders over $100.00

We ship UPS in the continental United States. We ship standard mail to P.O. boxes. Orders shipped to Alaska, Hawaii, The Virgin Islands, and Puerto Rico are sent first-class mail. Orders shipped to Canada and Mexico are sent surface mail.

International orders: Airmail—add freight equal to price of each book to the total price of order, plus $5.00 for each non-book item (audio tapes, etc.).

Surface mail—Add $1.00 per item.

Allow 2 weeks for delivery on all orders.
Postage and handling rates subject to change.

DISCOUNTS
We offer a 20% discount to group leaders or agents. You must order a minimum of 5 copies of the same book to get our special quantity price.

FREE CATALOG
Get a free copy of our color catalog, *New Worlds of Mind and Spirit*. Subscribe for just $10.00 in the United States and Canada ($30.00 overseas, airmail). Many bookstores carry *New Worlds*—ask for it!

Visit our web site at www.llewellyn.com for more information.

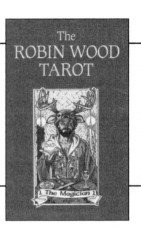

THE ROBIN WOOD TAROT
Created and illustrated by Robin Wood
Instructions by Robin Wood
and Michael Short

Tap into the wisdom of your subconscious with one of the most beautiful tarot decks on the market today! Reminiscent of the Rider-Waite deck, the *Robin Wood Tarot* is flavored with nature imagery and luminous energies that will enchant you and the querant. Even the novice reader will find these cards easy and enjoyable to interpret.

Radiant and rich, these cards were illustrated with a unique technique that brings out the resplendent color of the prismacolor pencils. The shining strength of this tarot deck lies in its depiction of the minor arcana. Unlike other minor arcana decks, this one springs to pulsating life. The cards are printed in quality card stock and boxed complete with instruction booklet, which provides the upright and reversed meanings of each card, as well as three basic card layouts. Beautiful and brilliant, the *Robin Wood Tarot* is a must-have deck!

0-87542-894-0, boxed set: 78-cards with booklet   **$19.95**

To order, call 1-800-THE MOON
Prices subject to change without notice

SHAPESHIFTER TAROT
D. J. Conway and Sirona Knight
Illustrated by Lisa Hunt

Like the ancient Celts, you can now practice the shamanic art of shapeshifting and access the knowledge of the eagle, the oak tree or the ocean: wisdom that is inherently yours and resides within your very being. *The Shapeshifter Tarot Kit* is your bridge between humans, animals, and nature. The cards in this deck act as merging tools, allowing you to tap into the many different animal energies, together with the elemental qualities of air, fire, water, and earth.

The accompanying book gives detailed explanations on how to use the cards, along with their full esoteric meanings, and mythological and magical roots. Exercises in shapeshifting, moving through gateways, doubling out, meditation, and guided imagery give you the opportunity to enhance your levels of perception and awareness, allowing you to hone and accentuate your magical understanding and skill.

1-56718-384-0, $29.95
Boxed kit: 81 full-color cards, instruction book

To order, call 1-800-THE MOON
Prices subject to change without notice

TAROT JOURNEYS
Adventures in Self-Transformation
Yasmine Galenorn

The tarot has long been used for divination, but now you can use it to guide your growth and change. *Tarot Journeys* offers a complete guided meditation, or lyrical story, for each of the twenty-two cards of the Major Arcana, which will teach you more about each card than you thought possible. Come to understand the spiritual nature of the energy behind each archetype, as well as the ways in which it relates to the cycles of your life.

Like the journey of the Fool (the first card of the major arcana), *Tarot Journeys* will guide you through the major choices and cycles that face everyone—from choosing a life-path to love, from personal sacrifice to shoring up self-esteem, from coping with the material world to searching for inner spirit. The meditations flow like classic fables, leading you through exotic imaginary lands, and guiding you into unexpected encounters with mythical people and creatures.

- includes audio CD with selected meditations from the book

1-56718-264-X, 288 pp., 7 ½ x 9 ⅛ $19.95

TAROT PLAIN AND SIMPLE
Anthony Louis
with illustrations by Robin Wood

The tarot is an excellent method for turning experience into wisdom. At its essence the tarot deals with archetypal symbols of the human situation. By studying the tarot, we connect ourselves with the mythical underpinnings of our lives; we contact the gods within. As a tool, the tarot helps to awaken our intuitive self. This book presents a thoroughly tested, reliable, and user-friendly self-study program for those who want to do readings for themselves and others. It is written by a psychiatrist who brings a profound understanding of human nature and psychological conflict to the study of the tarot. Tarot enthusiasts will find that his Jungian approach to the card descriptions will transport them to an even deeper level of personal transformation.

1-56718-400-6, 336 pp., 6 x 9, illus. $14.95

To order, call 1-800-THE MOON
Prices subject to change without notice

TAROT:
YOUR EVERYDAY GUIDE

**Practical Problem Solving
and Everyday Advice**

Janina Renee

Whenever people begin to read the tarot, they inevitably find themselves asking the cards, "What should I do about such-and-such situation?" Yet there is little information available on how to get those answers from the cards.

Reading the tarot for advice requires a different approach than reading for prediction, so the card descriptions in *Tarot: Your Everyday Guide* are adapted accordingly. You interpret a card in terms of things that you can do, and the central figure in the card, which usually represents the querent, models what ought to be done.

This book is especially concerned with practical matters, applying the tarot's advice to common problems and situations that many people are concerned about, such as whether to say "yes" or "no" to an offer, whether or not to become involved in some cause or conflict, choosing between job and educational options, starting or ending relationships, and dealing with difficult people.

1-56718-565-7, 312 pp., 7 ½ x 9 ⅛   **$12.95**